Spiritual Compass

Practical Strategies for When You Feel Lost, Alone and God Seems Far Away

Sue Hannibal

Foreword by Benedict Masilungan, M.D.

ISBN: 978-0-9969771-1-1

Guided Healing and Associates

Vista, California

Disclaimer: The information in this book is educational in nature, is provided as general information only and is not medical or psychological advice or diagnosis of any illness, disease or condition. The author is not a licensed mental health clinician or a physician nor does she practice psychology or medicine and does not diagnose mental, emotional or physical illness. She is an intuitive energy healer, medical intuitive, and spiritual coach. Sue Hannibal does not accept responsibility or liability whatsoever for any use or misuse of the information contained here or in the appendix, resources or web site links.

Dedication

To the Holy Spirit, who has guided and protected me on this sometimes perilous journey, and to my clients, who have trusted me with the sacred responsibility of holding their pain in my hands. Thank you.

Contents

The Daylily Prayer

Lord, let me be as the daylily;
let me open to the promise of each new day,
then die to the old
and bloom again,
renewed,
tomorrow.

i. Foreword

Over the course of two decades of private practice as an integrative physician, I've treated, mentored, coached and counseled thousands of patients. I've also, the author informs me, functioned as a "spiritual compass" for her for over 17 of those years. You'll likely see yourself in the pages of this fascinating book that is part memoir, part spiritual guidebook and part doorway to uncharted states of consciousness that produced profound healing for people who had been unable to find it anywhere else.

Sue Hannibal was referred to me in 1997 at the beginning of a spiritual awakening that required years of deep healing through the archetypal journey of the Wounded Healer. I have assisted hundreds of patients who have struggled, as she has, to regain their balance when their life has been "turned inside out." Sue initially presented, as many people do, with depression over the breakup of a marriage and was desperately seeking guidance. Her intuition, which we are all born with, gradually emerged to guide her as well. Intuitive abilities come in a variety of styles and levels of power. You'll will learn the value of acting on, and in one passage the dangerous result of *not* acting on, their own intuition.

In Part I, those seeking direction in an increasingly stressful, anxious world may find it in 38 channeled essays which express universal spiritual principles. Others who may find themselves in a personal or spiritual crisis will find illumination in the one-size-fits-all wisdom.

In Part II, you gain rare access to the healing room where they witness scenes of supernatural phenomena as well as the transformation of physical, mental, emotional and spiritual issues that in some cases had persisted for years. This volume will empower you to investigate integrative medicine and holistic healing, especially those still searching for solutions due to the limitations of western medical, psychiatric and psychological approaches. The true case histories profiled here, for example eight years of panic attacks in an Army officer that were rooted in his traumatic birth, will demonstrate to readers (and I hope to some of my medical and psychiatric colleagues) that thinking outside the box is allowed if the treatment is effective and does not harm.

Since 2004, Sue has taught hundreds of students, including licensed mental health clinicians, to "read energy" so they can intuitively diagnose the hidden roots of trauma, whether they find the roots in this dimension or the next. As she says to her therapist students, "Who can define the timeline of the soul? If tracing the energetic signature of trauma leads to a traumatic birth, the womb or a past-life and releasing that brings healing in present time, don't wring your hands over it, just do it."

Many healers cannot teach and many teachers cannot heal. Sue can do both.

As in any true story, the vulnerability and courage required to reveal personal details makes this a compelling read. By telling her story from her heart, Sue encourages you to jettison fear, take up their own spiritual compass and follow the calling of their own heart.

Benedict Masilungan, M.D.

"One can't believe impossible things," Alice said. "I daresay you haven't had much practice," said the Queen. "When I was your age, I always did it for half an hour a day. Why, sometimes I've believed as many as six impossible things before breakfast."

Alice in Wonderland

ii. Preface

People have been seeking answers to the questions "Why am I here?" and "Why is this happening to me?" since God allowed Satan to put his upright and blameless servant Job to the Biblical test.

If you're like me and the thousands of clients who have come to me for intuitive healing, your life has been scarred by trauma. It could be from childhood abuse or neglect, illness, grief and loss, going to war, a financial reversal—the list is nearly endless. My journeys through survival of a traumatic life-threatening birth, childhood trauma, depression, divorce, life-threatening illness, betrayals and abandonment by people I loved and trusted and various terrifying brushes with death, have tested my faith and stretched my resilience beyond what I ever thought possible.

The emotional, spiritual and/or physical suffering that visits each of us eventually leads either to despair and addiction or to the search for self, healing, meaning, empowerment, forgiveness of self and others and a renewal of faith and connection to God. At a particularly frightening point in my own journey, when life collapsed around me in the space of about two weeks at age 43, I found myself alone on my knees, depressed, scared and crying out to God as human beings have since the dawn of humanity: "What is going on?" "Why are You doing this to me?"

I received an answer--lots of answers. They came to me as channeled reports from the spiritual front dictated by my angelic assistants nearly every evening between 1999 and 2000. I've combined these messages with stories of trauma, struggle, pain and finally healing of my clients as well as myself. As the last grains of sand slipped through the millennium hourglass, I wondered why I had been chosen to receive these messages of timeless wisdom, practical strategies for living and shoot-from-the-hip spiritual truth.

I didn't know it at the time but I was about to enter a period of spiritual depression followed by the growth and renewal St. John of the Cross called "the Dark Night of the Soul."

Navigating the Dark Night Without a Compass

When we enter the Dark Night, we're forced to confront what we've always believed or how we've always behaved ("If I take care of others they'll take care of me...") but which no longer serves us and then discard that like a coat that no longer fits. Along the way we endure a painful pruning process that, like trimming branches in a fruit tree, yields a more bountiful harvest.

When life drives you to your knees in a spiritual, emotional and sometimes physical metamorphosis, among your choices are alcohol, drugs, suicide or faith. As soon as I gave up fighting, released my desperate grip on my old life and shifted from fear to trust, miracles began to happen. God threw me a faith lifeline and everything changed. Fear faded as doors opened, provisions and supportive people appeared and spiritual gifts emerged.

If you've lost your compass in the spiritual wilderness like I did, you'll have to look up to access your backup navigation system. Teachers, healers and talking heads on TV come and go but God is like the North Star. The loving, creative energy that is God doesn't have a gender, but for clarity I'll use "He." God is permanently accessible 24/7 and His guidance is accurate no matter where you are and where you come from. Universal truth (do not murder, do not steal, treat others as you want to be treated) can be found in any sacred text. Universal truth is a lot like gravity; it's one-size-fits-all and applies everywhere equally whether you decide to believe in it or not.

Spiritual Compass is a joint effort, co-produced by the Holy Spirit. This collection of spiritual essays covering "Life 101" is rich with wisdom, guidance, encouragement and support for living a full life at the intersection of body, mind and spirit. They have comforted, intrigued and guided me and my clients to stare down our worst fears. I hope they will do the same for you.

Even in the midst of my darkest moments, if I was still and listened, I could sense the gentle presence of spiritual support. Perhaps like you, I've pondered the concepts of universal spiritual truth vs. man-made religious doctrine and dogma. I was raised Catholic. Through my youth and into my 30s, I was indoctrinated more about sin, punishment, hell, penance and the man-made rules and regulations of various denominations than the loving, eternally forgiving nature of God. In my 30s I embraced the born-again Evangelical Christian movement for several years. In my 40s, as Spirit spoke to me through direct guidance, prayer, dreams and these channelings, the narrow interpretation of Biblical "truth" and the controlling nature common to the doctrines preached in so many conservative churches just didn't fit anymore. I commenced a search for a direct spiritual connection that would embrace my expanding consciousness and met a lot of fellow dropouts from other mainstream religions at Unity, Unitarian Universalist, Religious Science and other non-denominational gatherings.

I respect all religions (other than Satanism and any form of black magic or evil that has been repackaged as a "religion") and view all names of God as paths to the same divine Source. I consider anything negative that is done or said in the name of God that harms, enslaves or otherwise attempts to control another human being to be a manifestation of evil. Communion with God is a state of being. It is a knowingness much like being connected to an electrical circuit that is always on. Jesus said as much in his gospels about seeking God's face and His will for our lives.

Now that I've spoken directly to Spirit and Spirit has spoken back quite eloquently, there's no doubt in my mind that the spiritual laws are universal. They're as dependable and as logical as gravity. They function everywhere for everyone regardless of belief and they *always* work. In fact, they're so dependable that trying to ignore them is like trying to ignore gravity. A law that everyone has experienced is the law of cause and effect, also known as what you sow, you shall also reap, what goes around comes around and the golden rule: do unto others as you would have them do unto you. Spiritual laws (aka natural laws) transcend race, gender, age, nationality, culture, politics, religion and borders. If you're on this planet, these laws apply to you and the sooner you understand them and begin to work within them, the easier and more prosperous your life will become.

This book will not guarantee delivery of the love of your life, wealth, power, health and a beach house but it will save you from a lot of suffering if you decide to apply the universal wisdom in these channeled messages, which I continue to receive to this day. However, if you find yourself in the middle of your own Dark Night, allow the wisdom, comfort and practical strategies in these pages to illuminate your path and deepen your faith as they have for me and my clients. I pray these writings inspire and empower those of you who seek healing and guidance to find it in the voice of God.

With Love,
Sue Hannibal

Vista, California
www.suehannibal.com

Part I
Appointment with Destiny

"When the other person is hurting, confused, troubled; anxious, alienated, terrified; or when he or she is doubtful of self-worth, uncertain as to identity, then understanding is called for. The gentle and sensitive companionship of an empathic stance provides illumination and healing. In such situations deep understanding is, I believe, the most precious gift one can give to another."

Psychologist Carl Rogers

Introduction

A channeled message: August, 2004

Dear Susan,

We are here for you as always. You ask us for guidance and we are glad to give it to you and to support you as you go through this transition. The questions are not as important as the answers, and we will assist you in finding the answers that you seek for your own growth, happiness and health.

First you are wondering about why this awakening is happening at this time. You are being prepared to take on even greater responsibilities and duties in the Holy realms. The time has come for you to step up to the plate, as you are fond of saying, and grapple with issues that have bothered you all your life. This old baggage slows you down, makes you sad, takes your energy and attracts people who are not in a high vibration. You have important work to do and so this healing must take place at this time to purify your intentions and get you back on the center track of Spirit. Your fears are groundless. You are divinely provided for and cared for. This time of rest, introspection and rebirth is necessary and you will benefit greatly from it. This clearing will move your work to a higher level and will be reflected in your upcoming book on healing. That book needs to be of a high spiritual vibration, to carry the weight of the truth it is to convey to the masses. People will literally be healed by this book. It will validate for the first time for some that the journey of pain, deprivation and loneliness that so many people live inside every day can end in healing.

After 16 years of private practice treating trauma and doing medical intuitive readings and channeling spiritual guidance for myself and thousands of clients, I'm offering the same spiritual compass that has guided us to guide you. A compass is a guide and a navigation tool. It doesn't take you where you want to go; it shows you the direction you need to go to get there yourself. This book doesn't tell you what to do or how to get there. Rather, it's a guidebook of spiritual wisdom and universal truths that will help you decide for yourself what to do and how to get there on your own. As with any journey, how you get there, which path you take and how long and arduous is the trip is up to you.

As we tread water in a sea of terrorism, violence and racial hatred, some people turn to faith for guidance and others blame God for the darkness in the heart of humanity.

Fortunately, there are people everywhere who care about others; they lift cars off trapped pedestrians, back up a police officer fighting a suspect or catch children thrown from a burning building. For every predatory criminal, there are dozens of open-hearted people who work with the homeless, at-risk youth, the elderly, prison inmates and abandoned animals.

In this book I've combined the menu of channeled guidance on a variety of topics with which we all struggle with practical wisdom and practical strategies for personal navigation in an increasingly scary, uncertain world. I intend for this shoot-from-the-hip collection to have universal appeal no matter your religion, culture, age, gender or any other demographic. The fact is, when you're about to set off on a life-changing journey, you need a map and a good set of directions—and if you're lost in the physical, emotional or spiritual wilderness, you'll need a compass.

In case you can't find your compass right now and you're feeling abandoned, depressed and scared, you can borrow mine. Suffering is not something a healthy person intentionally cultivates but it's frequently a necessary component of spiritual maturation. Entering (or being forced into) a classic Dark Night spiritual crisis usually brings depression, self-assessment, accountability, awakening and then ascension. Caroline Myss, one of my favorite spiritual teachers and a medical intuitive herself, calls the Dark Night experience "spiritual madness." I agree.

"And the day came when the risk it took to
remain tightly closed in a bud was more
painful than the risk it took to bloom."

~ Anais Nin

Chapter One: Nowhere to Look but Up

As I entered my 40s, I didn't know that the visionary and intuitive abilities I'd brushed aside for years were about to be expanded, refined and tested. It was apparently time for my life purpose to be fulfilled. I never meant to become a healer but apparently God had a different idea. In the space of about two weeks in the summer of 1997, I found myself yanked out of a sixteen year marriage, my home, job and life as I knew it. When the dreadful spinning stopped briefly, I found myself face to face with my biggest fear—the fear of being alone, which I later learned was rooted in the survival level fear of abandonment. Like a whirlpool in a deep river, I was being helplessly drawn into the classic "Dark Night of the Soul" spiritual crisis that would put me on a collision course with my spiritual destiny.

For years I pretended my second marriage was happy because if I admitted, even to myself, how miserable I really was, I might actually have to do something about it. The wounded child inside me wanted to continue living in the illusion that she was safe and being "taken care of." The reality was I was taking care of myself, my emotionally abusive husband, publishing and editing a national newsletter, writing a column for a national magazine, helping to run a business plus handling the majority of the tasks of daily living. The unrelenting stress of juggling two lives was siphoning the life right out of me.

Garden-variety selfishness in a spouse is merely irritating. Living with a narcissist is dangerous to a partner's health. About a month after I left him, "Jake" called to inform me that he'd had a talk with God and knew why our marriage was in trouble. I said, "Really. I can't wait to hear what God had to say." In typical narcissistic fashion he announced, "If only you'd stop complaining everything would be fine."

Even after that revealing but not unusual exchange, I was still terrified to be on my own. The daily bouts of stomach-churning anxiety and clinical depression made me feel like I was drowning. I couldn't advocate for myself and no one realized I needed a therapist. I sank to the bottom of a dark abyss and lay there in the spiritual vacuum waiting for rescue. The lifeguard never showed and there was nowhere to look but up.

Eventually denial kicked in and I had a little "grass isn't greener" pep talk with myself, rationalizing that nobody is perfect, marriages take work and at least he wasn't hitting me. I didn't yet connect the dots between my failing health and staying in a dead, emotionally toxic marriage. I didn't yet know that where I'd been didn't have to be where I was going. I remember worrying one lonely, sleepless night, "If I leave him, what if I'm driving home some rainy night and I get into an accident? No one will know I'm missing."

Crisis of the Self

A few days later, I headed for the beach on a perfect October day. As I approached my favorite expanse of sand, a van pulled up and offloaded a man who appeared to be a paraplegic in a motorized wheelchair. The van drove away and the man sat there alone, gazing out at the ocean. My eyes filled with tears at the sight. Here I was feeling sorry for myself, angry at God, furious with my self-absorbed abusive husband and this poor man who could barely move a muscle was sitting there smiling at the sun.

I walked over and said "Hi." He smiled and replied enthusiastically, "Hi! How are you on this beautiful day?" My sunglasses couldn't hide the fresh flood of tears.

He said softly, "Why are you crying? What's wrong?"

I sat on a boulder and gathered my knees to my chest.

"I'm getting divorced and I'm scared of the future. I don't know how I'm going to survive."

He leaned forward and gently patted my leg.

"Look, I know this seems really bad right now but you know, it could be the best time of your life."

I was so taken aback we just looked at each other for a moment.

"How do you do it? You're stuck in this chair, dependent on others for everything, yet you're here, smiling and comforting me. I envy you."

He smiled up at me. "It's not so bad. I have a lot to be grateful for. I can come here and be near the water, watch the birds and sometimes nice people like you come up and talk to me. I'm a lucky guy."

I stared out at the crashing surf, feeling smaller and more ashamed with every word. Here I was bitching and whining about my life, grateful for nothing, yet somehow, I can only guess it was grace, this paraplegic man in his 30's had peacefully accepted the cards fate had dealt him. I never saw him again but I'll never forget him.

The crisis of the "self" confronts all of us at one time or another. Illness and accidents that strike us or loved ones can blindside us. For some, mid-life is when the walls seem to close in. Children are leaving the nest, bodies are aging and the health and vitality that we once took for granted must be carefully nurtured and protected. Relationships collapse, loved ones die and financial security becomes a concern as retirement approaches. What always worked for us, what was always there, may no longer be dependable. It can shake us to the core.

With this divorce, my own "crisis of the self" had begun and God was there, every faltering, terrifying step of the way, even when I wasn't aware of His steadying hand on the chaos my life had become.

I'd written my way out of life crises before so I started a journal.

"Day 3. Before I can write a word of this experience—the adjectives come haltingly—wrenching, sad, freeing, regret, peace, focus on self, destiny, acceptance. It sounds like the grief process when a loved one has died. There has been a death here, of my marriage and my illusions. The first night I ever lived alone in my life was Saturday. For weeks, I agonized over all aspects of the decision: stay or go, now or later, what will happen to him if I go, what will happen to me if I stay? I look around at all my lovely, familiar things with all the memories attached, boxes of stuff everywhere and in the midst of it all a peace and a feeling that somehow, in the midst of all this chaos, this is where I belong. I don't understand quite how I got here but I have placed my trust in the Lord and am learning to take one day at a time.

My subconscious continues to speak to me. Last night I dreamed that I was cracking eggs open for breakfast and as I looked into the bowl, tiny human embryos in various stages of development slid out of the eggs. When I woke up, the dream was very vivid and I knew that it was a symbol of re-birth—of myself. According to Sigmund Freud and a book on dream interpretation, "The egg represents 'Genesis'—beginnings. The egg, properly fertilized with the creative force and incubated, germinates new life. In a dream, this might be a new project, a new phase in life or a new sense of self."

The memories of those early days alone are still vivid. In the space of two weeks, life as I knew it imploded and took my identity with it. I was no longer a wife, no longer half of a partnership—even a destructive, unhealthy one. I was co-owner of an automotive business and I had to leave the business, so I was out of a job. I had to quit writing my column for the national automotive magazine I'd been part of for three years and had no idea where I would find another job.

I wrote:

The fear and dread is so heavy it feels almost physical, as if I'm being squeezed and pushed into a place that seems smaller than I am. At times the anxiety takes my breath away and the pressure on my chest makes me gasp for air.

And this entry a few months later, looking back:

The constant, draining, low-level dread only left me for the few hours when I finally fell into an exhausted sleep. Each miserable day felt as jarring and shocking as the sensory overload of birth must be to a newborn. I was terrified for three months. I craved sunset because that meant I'd made it through another day. I dreaded dawn because it meant another day of struggling to survive the battles with fear, exhaustion, grief, loneliness and pain.

Whoever coined the term "heartbreak" knew what they were talking about. My heart hurts. It aches. It feels cracked in a dozen directions, held together by virtue of a continuous pattern of beats. This depression is a bottomless cavern of pain and blackness. It's like being only half dead. You're not dead enough to be free of the pain and not alive enough to rise up and throw it off. It's the worst kind of suspended living I know of.

It's All in the Cards

My first attempt to wrestle back some control over my life in the spiraling chaos it had become was to consult an astrologer. I thought dully, "Maybe all this pain has a purpose. Maybe it's in my chart." I was grasping for control, desperate to find some reason, some clue that the collapse of life as I knew it was part of a larger plan. I sat down with the astrologer and demanded to know why my life was unraveling and how to stop it.

She smiled indulgently, gesturing to my natal chart and the spread of tarot cards beside it. After a dramatic pause she announced, "Chiron, the archetype of the Wounded Healer, is at the top of your chart, at 12:00. You're here to be a master healer, spiritual teacher and a bridge for others between body, mind and spirit."

As she regarded me over the top of her glasses, I sifted this rather startling revelation through my brain, seeking a definition of "healer" that I could comprehend. Finding none, other than a physician, and knowing I wasn't going to medical school, I drew a blank.

"What's Chiron and what's a healer?"

She patiently explained that according to ancient Native American prophecy, when the planet of healing is discovered in the sky, the sacred warrior teachings will return to Earth. In astrology, Chiron's message concerns health and disease and how they impact our spiritual journey. Disease, dysfunction and disorder as well as health serve as our teachers. They challenge us and guide our path on the return to Spirit, wholeness, consciousness, truth and love.

As Chiron's message unfolds in our lives, we begin a journey through our shadow to confront and transmute the qualities of ourselves we see as faults and weaknesses. The shadow is our wounded hard drive. It contains our negative emotional menu—prejudices, judgments, grudges, shame, blame, guilt, jealousy, greed, traumas, fears and all the painful experiences of our lives, our subconscious and our soul.

As I was attempting to digest all this, the astrologer's predictions became more specific. She said I would practice the art of laying-on-of-hands, develop profound psychic, intuitive and spiritual healing gifts and that I'd be in private practice in my own office within three years after going through "a tremendous amount of my own healing." I was stunned. As I drove home, I struggled to compare what I had just heard about the plans God apparently had for my life with the Catholic doctrine I was raised with.

I went to public school but every Monday afternoon the Catholic kids were released early to go to religious instruction at the church down the street. As early as third grade, I began to question 1960s vintage Catholic doctrine. I understood Jesus as the son of God, the Holy Trinity and the Christmas story but I intuitively rejected some of the other dogma as soon as I heard it. For example, at that time the church taught that because we are all born with "original sin," babies who die before they could be baptized were destined to go to hell. That didn't compute and I rejected that teaching immediately. I also decided that reciting the prayers on the back of holy cards thousands of times to ensure that the divine scorekeeper would reduce my purgatory sentence when I died was just as useless as being forced to write on a chalkboard "I will not talk during class" 100 times. I wasn't great at math but that just didn't add up in my eight-year-old mind. I also wondered why, when the priest would occasionally visit our class unannounced, Sister would instantly drop to her knees on the hard floor. After observing this divine phenomenon for a few months, I started thinking that must be what women were supposed to do when men entered the room. I reported what I had witnessed to my stay-at-home mother and asked her why she didn't get on her knees in the kitchen when Daddy came home from work. She gave me a strange look and told me to set the table for dinner.

Then one fateful Monday afternoon, Sister informed her class of impressionable third graders that we should all feel very lucky that we were born Catholic because the Catholic Church is the only true church and that all the non-Catholics were going to hell. I momentarily forgot what could happen to a child who questioned a nun in front of the class in the 1960s and my hand shot up. "But Sister, I think you must be wrong," I earnestly explained, ignoring the dark look that passed over her face. "My best friend Cindy is Jewish and my other best friend Linda is Protestant and I'm not going to heaven without them." I don't remember what happened next but at dinner that night I recounted the exchange to my parents and informed them that I wasn't going back to religious instruction. I'd had enough of the Catholic Church. My father raised his eyebrows and looked at my mother, which was never a good sign, but she patted my arm. "Well dear, if that's the way you feel about it, you don't have to go back." I was stunned but chalked it up to divine intervention. The following week the priest called my mother to lobby for my return to the flock, suggesting that parental correction would be appropriate for my outburst of unsanctioned critical thinking about the one true church. For some reason she never explained, my mother stuck up for me and I never returned to Mondays with Sister. (Maybe it was the nun getting on her knees episode.)

For all you baby boomer Catholics, it's not my intention to bash the Catholic Church or any religion. In fact, I'm a big fan of Pope Francis, the coolest Pope ever. For the record, I respect all Holy Books and mainstream religions (Satanism is NOT a mainstream religion) as different paths to the same God. I'm just telling you how early religious dogma shaped me so you can assess your own programming in that area.

"Fortunately some are born with spiritual immune systems that sooner or later give rejection to the illusory world view grafted upon them through social conditioning. They begin sensing that something is amiss and start looking for answers. Inner knowledge and anomalous outer experiences show them a side of reality others are oblivious to, and so being their journey of awakening."

Henri Bergson, "On Intuitions vs Intellect" 1907

Chapter Two: Spiritual Not Religious Meets Intuition 101

My initial college education and employment background had been law enforcement related. I wanted to be a cop. My first real job was in retail security, catching shoplifters and dishonest employees. I didn't know it at the time but as my Reiki teacher later explained, I was "scanning" or "reading energy" in order to ferret out the thieves from the legit customers. I stayed with the retail security gig for 11 years, making several hundred misdemeanor and felony arrests. It was exciting, fun, challenging and occasionally dangerous, which I loved because I'd rather be dead than bored. In New York State I had a concealed weapons permit, so I carried a revolver in a shoulder holster under my hoodie, getting into the occasional foot chase and a few memorable fights. My father bragged about his little girl's bravado to his fellow firemen and some cop friends, my mother was terrified I would get hurt and people who know me now can't believe I ever did any of that. Eventually rolling around on the ground wrestling thieves into handcuffs while ruining $30 jeans and $20 manicures began to get annoying. After suffering endless humiliation from my colleagues because one teenage shoplifter I chased when I worked in California got away on a horse, I began to think about changing careers.

Needless to say, when I ended up facing the astrologer in the fall of 1997, I didn't want to accept that God was going to re-arrange my life so dramatically but as she spoke about being called as a healer and spiritual teacher, her words struck a chord somewhere deep inside me. It occurred to me that through the astrologer, God had answered my tearful middle-of-the-night pleas: "What is going on? Why are You doing this to me?"

The Awakening: Reiki

"There is no coming to consciousness without pain. People will do anything, no matter how absurd, in order to avoid facing their own Soul.

One does not become enlightened by imagining figures of light, but by making the darkness conscious."

C.G. Jung

Towards the end of the session, the astrologer recommended Reiki training as a good first step on my newfound healing path. After leaving her office, I was depressed, confused and scared. I still wasn't sure that God was in fact behind all this and I needed "proof" before buying into this Reiki thing. Reiki is a universal life-force energy healing technique that anyone can learn. I asked God for a sign that it was His will for me to be a healer.

After deciding to follow the astrologer's guidance, a few days later, I reported to the Reiki Master to begin my training, which I thought would be a short course in laying-on-of-hands but which turned out to be a year of intense training in healing and intuition that opened the door to my entire spiritual awakening. After taking a few Level One classes, the Reiki Master-Teacher does an "attunement" via laying-on-of-hands and attunes your body with the ability to channel and transmit the universal healing energy. It's similar to tuning the radio to your favorite station in order to pick up the signal. A Reiki student is supposed to have one attunement for Level One, another for Level Two and two attunements for the Master level. I've had dozens. My teacher was initially unable to get me out of my head and into my heart, so she just kept hooking up my energetic "circuits" with the Reiki attunements. She would try to explain the nature of spiritual healing and channeling energy saying things like, "This is something that you sense through your heart chakra." I would look confused and say to her, "What do you mean? Isn't there a book on this or a video?" Finally all the circuits connected and instead of being peacefully awake and aware, I became a walking satellite dish.

My teacher, I'll call her Jan, was a fifth generation clairvoyant, healer and medium from England. She welcomed me into her home, which I noticed was practically devoid of furniture other than a simple wooden table and two chairs in the kitchen. The heavy scent of sandalwood incense hung in the air. A bust of the Buddha held court on the fireplace hearth next to a 35-pound crystal shaped like a mountain range that reminded me of Superman's kryptonite. Next to that sat a molded shiny copper-pipe contraption shaped like a two-foot wide atom.

"Did you just move in?" I inquired.

"No, I don't use furniture," she replied with a smile. "We sit and sleep on the floor."

I smiled and nodded but I wanted to run out the door. Suddenly bickering broke out inside my head. "What are you doing here? You're nothing like this woman! She's probably some kind of witch or something. Get out!"

"No! You're here to learn unconditional love and non-judgment. She's your first teacher. You just stay right where you are."

Before I could decide which voice to obey, Jan motioned for me to follow and started up the stairs. We walked into a bedroom, empty except for what looked like a makeshift altar in the corner with several more sticks of incense poking up from a terracotta flowerpot filled with sand. She sat on the floor cross-legged and motioned for me to sit opposite her. Her eyes scanned the air above and around my head.

"I see that you'll be writing several books. You're here to be a master healer and teacher. You'd better invest in a good set of luggage because you'll be teaching and traveling internationally for your healing work."

I stared wordlessly at her, unable to believe this echo of the astrologer's matter-of-fact pronouncement.

The skeptic in me rejected her "reading." I thought, "She knows I'm an author, so she "sees" me writing more books—big deal."

Just then the doorbell rang, ending her impromptu look into my future.

Another Reiki student showed up for her attunement, which I was asked to stay and watch. I sat on the floor propped against the wall, while she began the prayers prior to the attunement. Suddenly I was overcome with a gentle wave of peace and relaxation so powerful I literally slid down the wall and ended up dreamily lying on my side on the carpet, eyes barely open. Jan glanced over at me and smiled. I may as well have been drunk. The energy in the room was so strong, yet gentle, that I nearly fell asleep. It felt like being bathed in love.

A succession of healers, a wonderful intuitive therapist and assorted spiritual teachers both physical and non-physical, have guided me on the journey back to myself. Most healers I know have been to hell and back in their childhoods and personal lives. Successfully navigating the ascension of consciousness thorough the archetype of the Wounded Healer seems to be a prerequisite for the sacred privilege of holding someone else's pain in your hands and guiding them through their own Dark Night of the Soul.

In the search for lost parts of myself, I decided to go back to the beginning.

The Babies

In October of 1997, after a depressing month of what felt like solitary confinement in my first apartment, the local paper ran an article reporting that the Polinsky Center, the San Diego County facility for abused and neglected children, was looking for volunteers. I signed up to volunteer in the baby cottage and spent many fulfilling hours taking care of babies and toddlers. My Reiki teacher later pointed out that I was drawn to the babies who had been taken from their mothers because I was temporarily taken from mine at birth. I was the youngest child of three and my mother was in labor with me for three days before they finally did a C-section, only to find the cord was wrapped around my neck. We both almost died. I was cared for in the hospital nursery for nearly three weeks, separated from my mother because she was struggling to survive the delivery. At one point she had a near-death experience, which she shared with me years later. Jan pointed out that the unhealed birth trauma and the weeks alone in the hospital nursery were perhaps roots of my anxiety and fear of being alone. Once I finished the volunteer training and started working in the unit, it did feel very comforting to feed, cuddle and rock the newborns.

Working with the babies further molded my intuition in a very primal way.

One day the staff was going to take a newborn boy to Children's Hospital because he wouldn't eat and was becoming dehydrated, which can quickly be fatal for a newborn. The mother had been breastfeeding when Child Protective Services took the baby and now he wouldn't take a bottle. While the staff were making arrangements, I said, "Give me the bottle; I'm going to try to feed him." They said they had all tried but I insisted, so they gave me a Playtex nurser and I took the screaming baby to a dark, quiet room in the nursery. I swaddled him snugly, then unbuttoned my shirt and cuddled him close with his face next to my skin so he could hear my heartbeat and feel and smell me. I gave him some Reiki energy and he began to settle, so I plugged the cheap imitation into his mouth. He quickly sucked down four ounces of formula. I burped him, brought him sleeping peacefully on my shoulder back to the staff and showed them the empty bottle. They demanded to know how I got him to eat, so I told them and left out the part about the Reiki. The snooty day shift supervisor threw a fit about my innovation being "against regulations." I shot back that I didn't care about regulations; it was the best thing for this baby instead of being dragged screaming to a hospital and having a nasal feeding tube shoved down his tiny throat. The other staff sided with me and she was silenced. She was hostile to me from then on but I ignored her.

Another time at Polinsky I walked in during the early evening. There had been a county-wide drug sweep the night before and the population swelled to over 32 babies. Extra cribs had been pulled out of storage and were lined up against the walls. Every baby was crying; it was a madhouse and the noise was deafening. I sat down at the manager's desk in the middle of the room, closed my eyes and fervently invoked Christ, the Holy Spirit and the angels of every baby in there to come to them and comfort them so they'd stop crying. Within about 10 minutes, the din died down and soon it was quiet. I had confided to one of the staff workers that I was a healer and was secretly giving Reiki to the babies. She casually walked over, looked around and whispered, "Was that you?" I nodded and we both burst out laughing, drawing strange looks from the other staff.

After a few weeks, the afternoon shift supervisor noticed how the babies calmed down and fell asleep when I held them and when I came in, she would give me the babies that were in distress. She was a very nice middle-aged Filipino woman. As soon as I appeared in the unit, she would call out in a sing-song voice, "Miss Sue, Miss Sue, I have baby for you!" Sometimes when the staff was shorthanded, she would beg me to stay and assigned one or two babies for me to take full care of. I would bathe, feed, change diapers, play, put them to bed, do the charting, etc. One time when they were really short-handed, I stayed for 12 hours. I gradually began to understand that being drawn to take care of the babies was healing for me and was helping me to reconnect with my own baby self that was still holding trauma from my rough birth.

Many of my clients have also had collateral damage from their time in the womb, a traumatic birth or trauma during infancy or toddlerhood that affects them profoundly in present time. Sometimes a traumatic birth can cause panic attacks of unknown origin. The feelings when the panic attacks come can be some combination of feeling like they're about to die, trapped, suffocating, stuck, terrified, claustrophobic, etc. Over 200,000 people go to the emergency room every year for what feels like a heart attack but which is actually a panic attack. Because conventional medicine and psychology aren't able to handle birth or womb trauma as a cause of panic attacks, they rule out a heart attack and send people home with some anti-anxiety medication until the next panic attack; then the whole scenario runs on auto-repeat. That's a lot of wasted health care dollars and resources. However, when the birth or womb trauma is healed using one of the energy psychology techniques, the panic attacks usually cease quickly as long as the root(s) of them are discovered and treated. Many people struggle with anxiety and a lifelong sense of sadness, rejection or worthlessness that traces back to being unwanted as a pregnancy or when one or both parents hoped for a child of one gender and the baby they expected was the other gender. Sometimes these encoded trauma imprints show up in a reading as rejection: "They don't want me, I don't belong here, I'm a burden, etc." The client then validates that thread of rejection and/or abandonment in their history.

One of the case histories in Part II tells the story of an Army officer who struggled for eight years with panic attacks of unknown origin, until we uncovered the very surprising hidden cause. The attacks resolved in one session. His case was the subject of a newspaper article in the September 25, 2008 edition of the *Fayetteville Observer* (North Carolina). More case histories about unusual psychiatric conditions such as Multiple Personality Disorder, now called Dissociative Identity Disorder, and some cases of apparent past-life trauma are in Part II. More stories are also posted on my web site, www.suehannibal.com.

"Any life career that you choose in following your bliss should be chosen with that sense that nobody can frighten me off from this thing. And no matter what happens, this is the validation of my life and action."

~ Joseph Campbell, The Power of Myth

Chapter Three: Visionary Sight in a Near-Sighted World

Most people, especially men, are more intuitive than they realize. One aspect of practical intuition is an expansive yet grounded way of assessing situations and organizations from a cause and effect perspective. That's a good definition of "reading energy" but it also works in reverse. One can assess the present effect or condition—fear, emotional trigger or behavioral pattern—and correlate it to unhealed trauma or neglect from the past. It recently occurred to me that some of the frustration I've felt much of my life is the result of visionary sight—a gift I've regarded as a curse for years. If you're a visionary too, it can be an enormous relief to know that you're not crazy or eccentric; your brain is just wired, shall we say, differently.

Visionaries think (and live) "outside the box." We sometimes get impatient when other people, especially bureaucracies and institutions, don't see the big picture as naturally and instantly as we do. Generally we're unconventional people. We prefer to get the job done our way because to us, it's clearly the most efficient way. That attitude can be risky. After getting fired a few times for making "suggestions" on how to streamline procedures at work, I stopped sharing the big picture. Non-visionaries accuse us of acting like superior know-it-alls but it's not our intention to be obnoxious. When you see the big picture, the blueprint of cause and effect, it's frustrating to be proactive instead of reactive, accurately identify potential pitfalls and negative outcomes, offer innovative, common sense solutions most people can't see and then be ignored. After the proverbial tree falls on the house, people don't want to hear, "I told you that was going to happen!" In the dangerous world we live in today, having a few select visionaries to advise high-level government and industry decision makers on how to plan their chess moves in advance would be a strategic asset. A lot of economic, social, environmental and military disasters could be avoided if more visionaries were advisors to those calling the shots. Visionary sight and intuition are crucial survival skills for children growing up in a war zone at home, or for soldiers in combat.

Visionaries are sometimes accused of being aloof by those close to us, although that's not a fair assessment. Actually since we're so expansive in our outlook, we care deeply about our family and friends and globally, about injustice, oppression and the corporate greed that's fueling the destruction of our environment. Visionaries observe the subtle manipulation patterns and propaganda inherent in politics, the media and the personal ego agendas of power brokers that may be difficult for others to discern. In other words, because we're good at sniffing out ulterior motives, we make outstanding management consultants, above-average jurors and general troubleshooters. We're big fans of proactive, common sense actions that get to the root of the problem. We abhor dumb rules and regulations in homeowners associations or "blue law" leftovers from the Puritans that restrict what one can buy and do on Sundays. We have no patience with passive-aggressive people, will go along with protocol if forced, wealth and status do not impress and we couldn't care less about people with big egos because they usually have narrow minds.

In 2012 the Navy commissioned a study on how to help soldiers improve their intuition but they gave the contract to some kind of left-brain consulting company which produced a uselessly complex death-by-Power Point with charts and graphs that couldn't help anybody discern the current time. I called the officer in charge of the contract, identified myself as a practicing intuitive and Army wife, attempted to offer him a few ideas that might actually work but he wouldn't talk to me about this unclassified public document. Your tax dollars at work.

Intuitive Guidance and Cause and Effect in Healing

Many clients have shared with me their intuitive experiences and dead-on accurate "hits" but they're afraid to tell anyone else. I want to de-mystify intuition here. It's not the work of the devil, it doesn't mean you're possessed by some sort of spirit and generally doesn't involve psychic predictions about what the stock market is going to do next. Intuition is a hard-wired natural ability available to us 24/7 just like any of our five senses. That's why it's called the "sixth sense." People all over the world, in every culture, social strata and in religious tradition have and use intuition.

Small children and animals are particularly tuned in to their intuitive guidance systems. Both tend to exhibit gut reactions that sometimes startle their parents and owners. A dog who observed a baby sitter abusing "his" baby alerted the parents who noticed his uncharacteristic aggressive behavior toward the sitter when she would arrive for work. That led them to leave a cell phone on record under the couch and they caught her abusing the baby. Parents of small children who don't want to go to daycare, or who resist contact with a family member, neighbor, family friend or ANYONE else, should recognize that resistance as a red flag and investigate carefully. If a child suddenly becomes clingy, starts wetting the bed, has nightmares or suddenly exhibits other unusual behavior in reaction to a person or situation, they're telling us "that person/situation is not safe" and/or "that person hurt or scared me." It's up to us to interpret and act on their signals.

Discernment and Intuition

When Jesus was asked how to discern whether a spirit was from God or the devil, he told the apostles to look at the outcome: "You will know them by their fruit." (Matthew 7:15-20 New King James Version). In other words, a person's motive and intention can be discerned by the outcome of their actions, as opposed to what they say. Some conservative Christians, including pastors, have rather suspiciously demanded to know "where I get my power from," referring to the ability to scan people's energy fields and do accurate intuitive readings. I told one Southern Baptist pastor, "I get it from the Holy Spirit." He countered, "How do you know it's the Holy Spirit?" I replied, "Because I use the same litmus test that Jesus taught for discerning truth when he walked the Earth. He said, 'You will know them by their fruit.' The pastor was not convinced.

I pray with each client before every healing session and my intuitive scans are consistently detailed and accurate. I believe that's because I invoke the Holy Spirit—the divine will—for my client. I ask to be told or shown whatever I need to know to help them, for their highest good and the highest good of all concerned and to be an accurate messenger for divine will for whatever healing or guidance they need. I set aside any expectations or judgments I might have, let go of the outcome and with a neutral mindset, wait to see what I'm given for them.

For the record, clairaudience, the spiritual gift of "hearing" subtle energies, or direct spiritual guidance such as channeling, has nothing in common with hearing voices due to schizophrenia, which is a severe mental illness in which the mind produces delusional visual and auditory hallucinations that "tell" the mentally ill person to do something like kill himself or harm others. There's no connection between schizophrenia, demonic possession and the expanded states of consciousness that accompany spiritual gifts/abilities of clairvoyance ("clear sight"), clairsentience (instant knowingness), being an empath (feeling someone else's emotions or physical pain in your own body) or clairaudience (intuitive "hearing").

Intuitive information comes in the form of subtle inner guidance. It doesn't tell you what to do, except in dangerous or life-threatening circumstances. It's never negative, obscene nor interferes with your free will. When visionary intuition and accurate, detailed spiritual guidance are applied to assess spiritual, emotional, psychological and/or physical health issues, it becomes medical intuition.

The Emergence of Spiritual Gifts and Heightened Intuition

After practicing Reiki for a few months and having dozens of attunements, various intuitive abilities began to surface one at a time and the ability to channel accelerated. Clairvoyance emerged first. My cousin came to visit in 1998, and one day I took her to the old Mission at San Juan Capistrano in Orange County, California. I sat on a bench in the huge courtyard admiring the myriads of rose gardens while she continued to inspect the exhibits. Suddenly a three-dimensional vision appeared before me in the center of one of the rose gardens. There were two brown-robed monks—one tall, the other a bit shorter—standing together facing me about 15 feet away. Their faces were hidden. The hoods of their robes covered their heads and they wore long belts of braided white rope. I stared, blinked, looked away, looked back and they were still there. Through the shock, I slowly realized I was sitting on holy ground, looking through a portal into another dimension of time and space. Tourists were walking about without comment. I also realized that although the monks looked three-dimensional to me, at the same time I could see through to the roses behind them. After about two minutes, they vanished. I was quite shaken and didn't even tell my cousin until months later. I did tell my Reiki teacher though. She calmly noted as she poured our tea that it was no big deal, that it was only my "third eye" opening up. It was a very big deal to me. I began to worry about what kind of supernatural phenomena I might witness next.

"Why is it that when we talk to God we're said to be praying, but when God talks to us we're schizophrenic?"

~ Comedienne Lily Tomlin

Chapter Four: Channeling is Taking Spiritual Dictation

Channeling was apparently next on the checklist of spiritual lessons. Jan explained the process to me as taking spiritual dictation from Christ, or a group of angels or a spiritual master from the Light. Her explanation didn't raise any red flags for me spiritually because there are dozens of references in the Bible of angels and archangels interacting with and delivering messages to people. An example is the Christmas story when the archangel Gabriel told Mary that she would be the mother of Jesus. Jan was careful to delineate channeling from the occult practice of automatic writing. At no time would I allow a spirit to take over my mind or body and speak or write through me. I agreed to be a spiritual court reporter and take the dictation, but that's all.

According to the research-based book *Channeling: Investigations on Receiving Information from Paranormal Sources* by Jon Klimo, channeling has an ancient history rooted in primitive cultures in Egypt, Japan, China, Greece and India and on into modern times. Channeling history dates to the Old Testament Bible and ancient Greece where even the priests communed with God to receive what they considered to be spiritual insights. Klimo defines channeling as "the communication of information to or through a physically embodied human being from a source that is said to exist on some other level or dimension of reality other than the physical as we know it, and that is not from the normal mind (or self) of the channel." He says the jury is still out on the question of the source(s) of channeled information. It can originate externally to the channel such as from a departed human soul in mediumship, a divine source or from an ability to tap into the Universal mind—what Carl Jung called the collective unconscious.

There have been various reports of what appear to be child prodigies who can paint like Van Gogh, Renoir and other old masters and it takes an art expert to tell the difference between their work and a priceless museum piece. Other children play musical instruments or write complex symphonies that are light years beyond the abilities they should have at their age. Let's face it, music lessons in grade school are wonderful for kids but the chance they'll end up playing Carnegie Hall is slim to none. So how can children do these things? The oft-quoted answer that channeling is a product of the channeler's own mind is clearly not possible in a child, although if you subscribe to the limitless unconscious, one could say that the child's unconscious mind is bringing forth this kind of genius. However, since most kids know nothing of tapping into the collective unconscious, that explanation doesn't fly unless the process is subconscious or energetic.

This kind of phenomena might be the work of the channeled souls of the art or musical masters but we don't have any way to measure or verify that. If we did, it probably wouldn't be done because that might prove the existence of reincarnation and the eternal nature of the soul. That data could cause the scientific method to collapse in a huge mushroom cloud and millions of dollars of grant money to evaporate faster than rain in the desert.

Nobody has yet been able to prove any of these paranormal theories. Perhaps at some point brain wave technology might shed some light on any differences in the structure or function of the brain of a channel or whatever is happening during the channeling process, but for now, no one really knows.

There appear to be various sources of channeled information as well as many styles of channeling. Some people, like the late American channel Edgar Cayce, the original medical intuitive whose thousands of health readings are catalogued at his institute in Virginia Beach, Virginia, do their readings in a sleep-like trance state. Others go into a trance so deep that another entity is able to take over and use their body to move and their voice to speak. This was the case with Jane Roberts, a teacher from upstate New York who channeled an entity who identified himself (if entities have gender) as "Seth. The Seth material, as it has become known, is a collection of 15 books of channeled information on a wide variety of topics that have sold millions of copies worldwide. Seth described himself as an "energy personality essence no longer focused in physical matter" and stated that he was independent of Roberts' subconscious. That's an interesting statement because many people believe that channeled information is just a stream of subjective information bubbling up from the channeler's own subconscious mind. Or, though intention, perhaps a channeler's subconscious mind enters a meditative or semi-meditative trance state that opens him or her to tap into the collective unconscious and download high-level universal truth and esoteric spiritual concepts from the higher realms.

A former California housewife named J.Z. Knight drew huge crowds in the 1970s and 80s when she channeled "Ramtha," identified as a 35,000-year-old enlightened soul from the lost continent of Lemuria who took over her body and voice to deliver his messages to packed lecture halls.

The Catholic tradition has a term for channeling spiritual guidance; they call it "interior locutions." In the evangelical Christian tradition, when the pastor or a member of the church stands during a service and begins to speak a message from the Holy Spirit, they call that bringing forth a "word of knowledge" which is acknowledged as one of the spiritual gifts in First Corinthians, a book in the Bible.

My experience of channeling is being wide awake, in control, consciously taking spiritual dictation. The information is direct, insightful, highly accurate, detailed and sometimes visual. The only information I have about any client prior to our first session is their name and age, whether they're in my office or on the other end of a phone or Skype connection somewhere in the world. The prayer we say before each reading is an invocation of perfect divine will for my client, for healing, restoration, protection, divine right action, peace, guidance, truth and whatever else we need. I've been careful from the beginning to never allow any entity to take over my will or my body and I decree that all information should come through the Holy Spirit guided by Christ. After that invocation, I feel a subtle shift in my energy that apparently prepares me to feel, hear, sense and/or see the information I'm about to receive about my client. It feels like a deeply peaceful, very calm, heightened sensitivity. I close my eyes, the information begins to flow and I start typing or writing by hand which generally takes about 30 minutes. Then we compare it to the "trauma timeline" the client gives me *after* I present the written reading to them. When we compare both documents, an accurate blueprint for self-healing and deep restoration emerges.

"What do you want with us, Son of God?"
they shouted. "Have you come here to
torture us before the appointed time?"

Matthew 8:29 New International Version (NIV).

Chapter Five: Spiritual Combat with Demonic Forces

A word of warning: there are some spiritually dangerous occult practices that can open one up to spiritual oppression and psychic/spiritual attack up to and including demonic possession. These include playing with a Ouija board, automatic writing, conjuring up spirits, black magic, voodoo, casting spells, witchcraft (not to be confused with Wicca, a pagan spiritual tradition that worships nature as God) and Satanism. Abuse of alcohol and/or drugs, sexual promiscuity and emotional trauma can also "tear" one's auric field, allowing negative outside influences to gain a foothold. In the case of playing around with black magic and the occult, that can sometimes be enough of an invitation to the dark side to walk in and stay until evicted.

I've had a number of paranormal experiences and adventures beyond the veil but I would describe the first one as hand-to-hand spiritual combat with evil that I'll never forget. I was going to do some energy healing work with a woman who was a licensed clinical social worker. She was referred to me for anxiety but when she showed up I learned there was paranormal activity in her house that was affecting her and her teenage daughter.

I had not yet begun to do formal intuitive readings but as we talked, I found myself clairvoyantly observing a pair of red beady eyes blinking at me from just above her head. As I was attempting to maintain a poker face and listen to my client while processing that I had apparently just made eye contact with a demon, my gaze shifted to her right shoulder. An ugly black claw that looked like one from a bird of prey with sharp pointed talons grasped her shoulder. As I was sifting this information, I remember thinking, "They're on her but not in her," because demonic oppression is not necessarily demonic possession. If it was a case of possession, I thought that would be revealed to me and I would discern the entities through her eyes and hear them through her words. As I mentally considered calling in Archangel Michael and Christ to dispatch these demons, I suddenly felt a light pressure around my head as a field of protective energy enveloped it. This force field extended out about 12 inches all around my head and it instantly reminded me of that big puffy turban Johnny Carson wore when he did the Karnac psychic routine. As I became aware of the energy "hat" encircling my head, a row of light beings which I assumed were angels lined up to form a protective barrier between us. I instantly discarded my plan to liberate her from the demonic oppression and instead told her what I saw and felt and asked her to come to an Anglican church I had recently joined which had a healing prayer service every Tuesday night. She agreed.

The following Tuesday my client, I'll call her Annie, showed up at the church with her daughter and almost immediately the demonic forces attached to them began to act up. I had told the pastor, assistant pastor and members of the deliverance and healing ministry what had taken place in my office, so they were ready. I was not. As the pastor and I were praying over, anointing with oil and laying hands on Annie's teenage daughter, her mouth opened and her tongue began darting in and out like the tongue of a snake. The horrified look in her eyes while this was happening told me it was involuntary.

After several minutes of prayer and anointing her with oil in the name of Christ, whatever was tormenting her left and she fell back into the pew weeping. Some women from the church comforted her while the team and I turned our attention to her mother. Annie sat in another pew and I stood behind her, both of my hands on her shoulders. Slowly her head began to shake side to side as if saying "No." I leaned forward to speak to her and see her face and as I did, the head shaking increased in speed and intensity. At the same time, her fists began to beat her knees and her feet were violently stomping the floor. I spoke her name over and over but she either couldn't hear me or couldn't answer. The rest of the prayer team left the people they were working with and came running.

We prayed over Annie and anointed her with oil in the name of Jesus of Nazareth for three full hours. Periodically the head shaking and foot stomping would cease and we thought it was over. At the direction of the Pastor I would ask her to recite the Lord's Prayer and she would begin but after a couple of verses she would be silenced again and the physical tantrum would resume. I scanned her head and body with my hands and each time felt an energetic blockage at her forehead.

Finally after three hours of intense spiritual battle when all of us were exhausted, whatever it was that had hold of her finally released. I scanned her field once again with my hand and didn't feel the blockage at her forehead. Although dripping with sweat and clearly spent, she was finally able to recite the Lord's Prayer to completion. Afterwards she explained to us that she was living with a man who was a heroin addict. The paranormal activity in her home and the entity attacks on her and her daughter began after he moved in. Needless to say, if I had naively taken on those demonic forces when I was alone with her in my office, all hell would have broken loose and I wouldn't have been able to handle it. Fortunately my angels intervened to protect me on that occasion and a number of others, some of which involved circumstances that were life-threatening to me or someone else.

There are dozens of scriptures referring to followers of Jesus having been given the spiritual authority through Him to deliver people from demons, heal the sick, even raise the dead but having said that, there's also a scriptural warning against putting God to the test through our own will instead of being directed by divine will. For example, the Christian cults which handle poisonous snakes during their services interpret a scripture literally that is clearly meant metaphorically. How do I know? Because numerous pastors who took it upon themselves to put God to the test in that way have died of snakebites. Please don't write to me with your perceptions that if they died that way it must have been God's will or He would have protected them.

I'm standing with "don't put the Lord thy God to the test." They were clearly operating from their own misguided free will and depending on scripture as an antidote. If you're sober and you are certain the voice of God is telling you directly to do something, it is probably not the voice of God if that directive would cause injury or death in line with the third dimensional laws that govern this planet. However God's power can indeed supersede those laws, one of which is that snake venom is normally lethal to humans. God is probably not the author of a directive to ignore gravity, and jump off a building. However He honors our free will, so blame yourself for exercising bad judgment if you make bad decisions, not God.

"I don't know what your destiny will be, but one thing I know: The only ones among you who will be truly happy are those who have sought and found how to serve."

~ Albert Schweitzer

Chapter Six: Channeling Messages from Spirit

After about a year of resisting my Reiki teacher's promptings to channel spiritual information because of fear, one night on the way to bed I was strongly guided to detour down the hall to my office and sit down at the computer. As I sat there with some trepidation, fervently invoking the protection of Christ, I "heard" a voice in my mind that appeared to originate from over my left shoulder.

"We're glad you're here. We've been waiting for you a long time."

That was almost enough to make me get up and run but I reluctantly stayed to see what would happen next. I squeezed my eyes shut and waited. Words began to form on a screen in my mind, and I began to type what I saw. I'd been a non-fiction author for over 15 years at that point and I knew I wasn't creating these words. They entered my mind and came out my fingertips as the rest of me observed from the side lines. The experience was like typing that line of text across the bottom of the TV screen when the station is running a news bulletin. First there was a short title, then the essay began to take shape as it would nightly for about the next year. The sessions usually lasted about 15-20 minutes, occasionally longer, and usually began with a title, then the words, "Tonight we wish to talk about..." The first one from the fall of 1999 is titled "Called."

At the end of the first session, I looked back over what I had just typed and sat there awestruck and a bit confused. Why me and why now, I wondered. I read and re-read the high voltage wisdom and comfort in these messages from heaven and decided to trust God and the process. I had apparently been chosen to carry these spiritual downloads and through Christ, I agreed to do so.

The main points of each essay line up with concepts of universal law and scriptural truth. They're positive, comforting, wise, sometimes blunt and timeless. I've since read many channeled books and have found that most channeled material has a very deep quality to it that usually has to be read in short bursts and then pondered or journaled about to let the timeless wisdom sink in. For that reason, I've never been able to read channeled books like a novel. The spiritual vibration that comes through to an awakened person is just too high to speed read and probably doesn't make much sense to someone who isn't on a spiritual wavelength.

After a while, I began to occasionally ask for guidance for myself. I didn't realize it at the time but doing the nightly channelings was like an internship at first, then a residency, training me to do detailed, accurate intuitive health readings years later in my private practice.

A few sample medical intuitive readings are included in Part II. I do them knowing only the client's name and age. I don't want to know anything about them or their issues because it's harder to discern what I'm getting from scanning them and what I know because they told me. The client can be in my office or on the other side of the Earth and accuracy isn't affected. The reading is not a psychic reading; it's a spiritually discerned assessment of the client's energy field, what the National Institutes of Health calls the "biofield" and the information is organized in writing according to the chakra system. Chakra is an ancient Sanskrit word for "wheel." Chakras, when viewed clairvoyantly or felt with a trained hand, appear to be circular energy vortexes that hold the imprints of traumatic memories and are connected like a complex freeway system to the body, brain, mind (which is separate from the brain) and the spirit. The reading forms a blueprint for our healing work, reveals the state of the client's emotional history and is linked to the impact of unresolved trauma on emotional, mental, physical and spiritual levels.

On a spiritual dimension, time, space and distance don't matter. Distance readings are still as accurate and easy, or in some cases easier, than in-person ones because if I can't see the client, nothing about their physical appearance can distract me. I only have the connection to their energy field and chakras and that allows me to survey them independent of interference by my other physical senses.

On a few occasions, I've presented a reading to a client and they report that most or all of it is not accurate. I've discovered there are a few reasons for that. One is that the information comes to me as a kaleidoscope of data, some of which is metaphorical that I have to interpret. For example, I might see imagery of an ocean liner listing on its side in the open ocean, which would be a metaphor for a client feeling as if their entire life is upside down. I also have to decide if what I'm seeing clairvoyantly is an actual event, such as a child being abused, or if that's a metaphor for someone who felt helpless and childlike in a situation.

In one case a medical colleague came for a reading and when I gave it to him, he said none of it was accurate. We went back and forth for a while trying to figure out if there was any connection at all to what I had picked up, which was a lot of information about being abused physically and emotionally. He denied any abuse and claimed to have had "a perfect childhood." I was about to give up and offer him a refund when he suddenly said, "Well, there was this one time when I was about five and my mother was trying to teach me to stay away from the stove, so she burned my hand with her cigarette lighter. Is that what you mean?" When I could speak again, I deadpanned, "Yes, I think we're onto something here." As we continued to work together, he eventually admitted that the reading was actually over 90% accurate but he didn't want to admit it.

Another time I was doing a phone reading for a woman and when I sent her the reading, she claimed that none of it fit her at all but it was 100% accurate for her husband. As we discovered after discussing their relationship, he was very emotionally dependent on her and was quite possessive and controlling. I then looked at his energy and could see it almost superimposed over hers, which she verified as feeling "smothered" by him. So when a person is joined at the hip emotionally with someone else—a child, spouse, parent etc.—their energy can become enmeshed and sometimes I can't sort it out. Co-dependency and blurred boundaries are not good for either party in that kind of a dance.

Here are the channeled essays in alphabetical order with some accompanying practical wisdom and practical strategies drawn from my personal spiritual journey as well as, at this writing, 16 years in private practice specializing in helping clients heal everything from past-life trauma to destructive emotional patterns. By applying the spiritual principles in these pages to your life and relationships, you will gain the benefit of having heaven as an advisor.

Called

Know that when you are called, you are being called into God's perfect will for you. Nothing you could possibly dream up or pursue out of your own power could possibly bring you as much satisfaction, joy, growth and opportunity to serve as being in God's will and walking in His light. "The eye has not seen nor the mind conceived what I have prepared for you," Jesus said. At the time, he was talking about heaven but he also meant heaven on Earth, in a state of grace in which one is literally creating heaven on Earth through service and alignment with God's perfect energy and will.

There can be no greater satisfaction of productivity than when one is being directed by the one who created you and wrote the directions for how to operate you. Who can know better what is best for you and your higher purpose than the mind of God?

So from now on, exercise your free will to make the best choice in your life path. Start with what it is you are good at or have an attraction for, whether it is underwater photography or elephant training. The world needs all of that and more. Know that God wants to co-create a perfect heaven on Earth with you and for you but He needs your permission. Step out and seek His guidance and you will be guided. It will have a certain right or familiar feel to it because you will be tuning in to the frequency of the seed that has already been planted within you—the seed of your own potential. You will need to identify it and then work with it to develop it into its fullest potential. You will be guided along the journey: people, books, classes—all the tools you need to reach your goal will come to you. Your goals must and will come to you if you are in God's perfect will. He will see to it that you have everything you need in order to fulfill your spiritual potential. You may not know how or when this is going to happen but you don't need to. That is what faith is all about. If God revealed his plans in advance, there would be no need for your faith.

So reach for the stars, dear ones. Expand your minds and dare to dream, for your dreams have power and they turn into desires and intentions, which are prayers that have caught fire. They are urgent demands for assistance from heaven and they will be answered. Then you and God can move forward in grace and confidence, fulfilling your contract with life and being the pebble that starts a ripple in a clear, mirror-finish lake... spreading outward and touching lives all around you, in ways large and small. Acknowledge the source. Plug your power cord into the most powerful outlet and watch the power flow. It will light up your life and power up your dreams beyond your own imagination.

Practical Wisdom: Tune into your heart, your deepest wisdom, and ask yourself: What do I really want to do, be or have? Or, what do I really want to get rid of in my life that no longer serves me? The heart reveals the longing of the spirit, the subtle call to service, creativity, goals—call it your inner bucket list. Even if you're not sure you can reach your goals, make the wish list anyway and tack it up on your bathroom mirror. Might as well let God know what you want so He can arrange for you to have it.

Practical Strategy: Self-diagnose any "stoppers" which are negative, limiting beliefs that can be felt as inner resistance and negative, fearful or limiting thoughts which are blocks to getting what you want. They will probably be rooted in parental programming that you were told or behavior that you witnessed, what you heard in school, church, culturally or in the mass media. Keep in mind that relentless anxiety-provoking media advertising such as the pharmaceutical cartels promoting a pill for everyone and everything, qualifies as propaganda. These invasive external belief systems and stoppers are virus programs on the operating system of your internal hard drive. They need to be neutralized and extracted for you to be able to achieve your goals, your best life and health. In the field of energy psychology, stoppers are blocks to healing or changing and are called "psychological reversals." These negative, limiting beliefs sabotage us and they have to be cleared, usually along with the traumas that imprinted them, before change or healing can happen. Trying to achieve a goal with active stoppers on your hard drive is like trying to run through deep water. It can be done but it's exhausting and slow. There's a list of common psychological reversals in the appendix.

Exercise: Pick one goal and write it down. Then close your eyes, place your hands over your heart and visualize in living color what it would look and feel like to have it already. Creative visualization and feelings through the heart center ignite manifestation, which is bringing thought into form. Thinking and wishing from your mind without a strong belief and positive expectation of delivery from your heart won't work.

If anxiety, negative thoughts, (i.e. "you don't deserve success,") come up or you feel resistance rather than a happy glow, write down the negative stoppers and where you feel it/them in your body. Maybe you'll recognize the words as something a parent, teacher or some other influential person said.

Use EFT tapping, Havening, TAT or another energy-based healing modality (see the RESOURCES section) to release the "stopping power" those negative thoughts and traumatic memories have over you. If you hit another wall of resistance or self-sabotage, (which is anxiety or fear,) realize that is just a virus program on your internal hard-drive. Write down the resistant thought or attitude, (i.e. "people won't like me and might abandon me if I'm successful") note where that limiting perception came from with the earliest root if possible. Notice where you feel the resistance in your body and rate the resistance or emotional charge on a 0-10 scale with 10 being the most intense. Print out the sample list of common psychological reversals in the Appendix and treat yourself for any psychological reversals, (blocks to healing or changing) that would prevent the issue from transforming. When you sense that the inner resistance is lessened or gone, treat yourself for the problem belief, fear or perception and the backstory behind it or find a practitioner to help you. There are dozens of YouTube videos showing practitioners in various energy-based modalities guiding clients through all sorts of emotional and/or physical issues. Watch some of them until you get the gist of how to do it, then try it on yourself. Don't pick the worst thing that ever happened to you to do alone, especially when you're just learning. Do the smaller, less emotionally intense issues by yourself, and take the most intense ones to an experienced practitioner either in person or by phone or Skype.

Coming World Events

The coming cataclysmic events in your world are not intended to destroy but to awaken. The earthquakes, floods and famines that are coming in these last days are the last outpouring of the Spirit on this world. God is waiting for men to turn their hearts to Him. God will not be denied. The oppressors of people in various parts of the world today will not stand against Him. His will is mighty and his sword sharp. God knows those that are His. He is not a respecter of religions, for religions are an invention of man. Religions are used to control people, even to the point of controlling the people's access to God, as if that were really possible.

People should not fear these words. They should go about the business of their daily lives but at the same time open their spirits to God and His word. Man was put on this Earth with a heart, a mind and a spirit. Just because he doesn't acknowledge his spirit doesn't mean it isn't there, waiting, ready to assist him with all of life's problems and concerns. This is the God part within us that will be there with us always, even after our physical death.

It is not our place to make predictions, for if the heart of man changes and returns to the fullness of the Spirit, the world can be changed as well. The forces of good and evil continue to wrestle over the hearts and minds of men. It is a galactic sized battle taking place on a very individual level, one soul at a time. Choose light, my friend, choose light.

Practical Wisdom: Anxiety is a modern epidemic. This message reminds us that even though we live amongst chaos and evil we can seek peace and stability in the spiritual truth that is found in all the holy books. Compared with just a few decades ago it's harder to feel safe in our homes, schools, on a plane or on the streets. Every time we turn on the news, there's something or someone to strike fear in our hearts, from fatal superbugs to super storms to flashes of violence. Some people try to protect themselves by avoidance but I don't recommend the "stick your head in the sand" approach to life.

Practical Strategy: Faith (trust) in God is a tried and true practical strategy. Invoking God's help and/or protection through prayer is available to all of us. The prayer doesn't have to be long and flowery. It can be "help me!" when faced with danger. Faith and prayer, combined with gratitude, are the power tools of creation and manifestation, which is thought-into-form. Discernment and critical thinking are tools everyone needs, what with fear being the primary ingredient of corporate, political and media propaganda to control the masses. Thoughts and intention backed by faith is spiritual power in action.

Gratitude expands, fear contracts. Affirm (declare) with gratitude and faith, that you're always safe under God's protection. Know that the universe acts on your prayers and intentions so be careful. You may not get what you prayed for but you will get what you intended.

As scripture says, believe that you have already received what you ask for. Conquer your fear by being a force for good in the world, whether it's by mentoring a confused, at risk teenager, volunteering to teach someone to read or just standing up for what you believe in.

Demystifying God and the Process of Manifestation

Tonight we want to talk about Spirit—the kind of Spirit that is limitless and vast, the kind of Spirit that confounds the mind of man. We understand that it is hard for you on the Earth plane to understand and fully comprehend the nature of God and Spirit. We wish to try to demystify God, so that you may partake in His fullness and grace more completely.

The nature of God is a formless yet powerful being of light, an energy if you will. This energetic being operates according to a different set of laws than those on Earth, so in other words, your human limitations, laws and expectations do not apply. The light and energy that is God cannot be explained in human terms using human language. But just as you do not see the wind but know that it is there, you see its effects. Know that in the same way God and Spirit are as real and powerful as the wind.

The way to engage the power of Spirit is to use the part of yourself that conforms to Spirit; the part that also has no physical form that you can see or feel or hear. Use your mind and the power and intention of your thoughts to give form to Spirit. For it is your thoughts and intentioned prayers that ignite Spirit to take form. When you pray, you are invoking Spirit to move, to change, to act, to take shape. Manifestation and alchemy are ways in which intention is applied to energy, thought or Spirit, to bring about something in physical form, such as physical healing.

This is the way to come to know the nature of God, through prayer. When Jesus said, "Cast all your worries on me," he meant tell me your worries, express your pain and give it to me to carry and transform for you. The act of confession helps one release a burden and lightens the heart. Whether or not the prayer is answered according to your preference does not matter. What matters is the confession, the expression of the desire or need. This is the first stage of healing. When you cry out to God to help change your circumstances, what you're really praying is, "God please change ME. Help me to be more loving, less judgmental, more patient."

God cannot wave a magic wand and do your bidding over another person. He cannot and will not do the same over you for that matter. When you are in conflict with another and you want God to intervene on your behalf, what you are really praying is to ask God for help so that you can find a way to better handle yourself and your own reactions and behavior.

You may not be happy to hear this but it is the truth. What consequence is it to you what happens to another person? You do not know their path or the lessons they are here to learn. You should be content to have your own reactions mitigated, so that you stay centered, in peace about the situation, and are able to detach from the pain, looking at the person's heart the way God does.

This takes spiritual maturity and a willingness to let go of trying to manipulate other people and circumstances for your own comfort or gain. It requires instead trust, compassion, patience and a great deal of faith. You have to be able to step back from a situation and say, "God, I know you have this entire situation well under control, and that you will work things out for the highest good of all concerned if only I would get out of the way and let you do it. I will remind myself once again that I may be seeing one channel on the cosmic TV, but you see the entire network."

If you find yourself grieving about a betrayal or loss of love, a circumstance that didn't work out the way you expected it to or any number of difficult human circumstances, know that God has not abandoned you or hidden His face from you for some real or imagined transgression on your part. He may be withholding giving you guidance directly, so that you are forced to exercise your faith, stretch your Spirit and seek out your path and the correct answer yourself. Again, this goes back to growth, which we equate with wholeness and healing. Everyone feels insecure or frightened at times and you are no different. But as the Wizard of Oz said to the tin man, the lion and the scarecrow, "You've got something they haven't got: faith, courage and your God-given brains." And it is in your hearts that you will feel the answer begin to form most of all. Your mind can confound you and lead you in a circle but when you know something from your heart, you know that you are on solid ground.

Practical Wisdom: People with histories of serious trauma sometimes have a difficult time sorting out their fears, trust issues and relationship with God. To a small child, parents are very God-like and God seems very parent-like. If a child is being abused or neglected by a parent, that can result in a faith crisis later in life. Examine any spiritual conflicts you have and see if they remind you of a relationship with a dysfunctional or abusive parent or another important person in your life who you feel has betrayed you.

Practical Strategy: Once when I thought I was praying but I was really whining about something, I received guidance through images and words as follows: when construction workers are preparing to pour a slab of cement to build a structure, the first thing they have to do is set the form on a solid, clean, level foundation. Then they pour in the cement and wait for it to set up. If they remove the wooden form before the cement is hardened, it will slide out in a formless mess. Then another scenario was shown to me. When we decide to place an order online, we select what we want to buy, put in the payment and shipping information and know that it will soon arrive. Unless we're neurotic, we don't call the 800# every day and bug customer service: "When is it coming? Is it on its way? Are you sure?" We confidently wait for the delivery and sure enough, it arrives. This is a metaphor for manifesting through prayerful intention and faith.

Pray for the outcome you want, be it healing, a new job, the right mate, whatever and soak in a sense of gratitude and joy because you've already received it even if you believe it's still in the shipping department.

Leave the delivery method and timing up to God. Just know that it's the perfect response to your request. And if the order doesn't go through and the prayed for outcome doesn't arrive? Maybe your belief that you wouldn't get it is stronger than the faith that you would. The universe hears the most powerful prayer, even if it's marinated in fear. Remember, what you put your constant attention on, you get more of. Make sure it's positive.

Fate

We wish to talk to you tonight about fate. People think that fate is predestined, as if they play no part in the way their lives unfold. This is not true. People come into your plane of existence with a job to do, lessons to learn and much capacity for good. Unfortunately people also have a capacity for evil, some more than others. Those that are more spiritually attuned seem to have an easier time because they are in touch with their reasons for being here. It is not a random accident of birth that you or any other person is here. Your part in this vast play has already been written and now you need to get onstage and play it out. Your role may be one of helper to another, leader, scribe, communicator, healer or many others. All are vitally needed and equally valuable in the big picture. God knows that the very hairs of your head are numbered. And He knows it when a sparrow falls to the ground. Each person on the Earth is here for a divine purpose. It may not seem so to look at the world today and the conditions in some parts of the world but we need more worker bees than queens. In the efficient world of the hive, every bee has its job. So when life becomes flat and seemingly without purpose, remember the worker bee. There would be no hive building or honey production without him.

Practical Wisdom: We are all, at our core, spiritual beings having a physical experience on Earth to fulfill the destiny of our soul. Everyone has a mission but whether we engage it or not is a function of our free will. So how do we recognize a spiritual call versus an ego decision to move, change jobs or run off to an ashram in India? In my experience talking with thousands of clients, teachers, students and friends about this, the most common signpost is that the mission involves a path of service to others, sometimes triggered by the need to learn lessons which move our soul journey forward. If we are in fact here to raise our spiritual integrity, then how better to gain compassion for others than having endured pain? How better to learn forgiveness than having someone trespass against us or someone we love? We live in a world of cause and effect, even if it's not immediately apparent. Einstein said, "For every action there is an equal and opposite reaction," or more commonly, "What goes around comes around." The Bible instructs us to "Do unto others as you would have them do unto you." Sounds like Einstein was explaining the ancient universal truths of karma and the golden rule through physics.

Practical Strategy: In the introduction to this book, my spiritual evolution began with my life being dismantled and being told by the astrologer and the Reiki teacher that my soul purpose was to be a healer.

> Look to your heart for the answer to the universal question: Why am I here in this space, time, longitude and latitude? For what purpose was I born? Is life just an accidental meeting of sperm and egg? Sometimes it looks that way but look deeper and you'll find the answer, or the answer will find you.

> Many historical figures who have made a huge impact on humanity, were born in less than ideal circumstances. So that being true, one could argue that the accident of birth is just the doorway, that a soul's purpose would end up being fulfilled (as long as one's free will is in agreement) without regard to the doorway used to enter this dimension.

Oprah Winfrey has said she always knew she was "destined for greatness." Her soul purpose, the expression of her destiny and path of the incredible force for love and good and healing that Oprah is, could not be subverted by the circumstances of her birth or the childhood trauma she has survived. The soul's purpose has a force of its own and can express itself in some of the most surprising and initially inconvenient ways. But when we look back at how our lives have unfolded, having been forced to walk through the fire of trauma and adversity and emerge purified at the other end, the puzzle pieces come together to allow us to see that our trials were part of the path all along. The next channeling continues this discussion.

Finding Your Life Path

The key to finding why you were put on this Earth is faith. God shows all of us our life avocations at different times in our development. Some avocations require more training than others, just as some professions require advanced studies and a degree and others do not. Frequently a prerequisite on your path will be "life experience 101." You will serve an apprenticeship in order to hone your practical skills that will serve you as you serve others later on. In order to deal with another person's pain, you have to know what pain is. This, for example, is how compassion is created in a soul. Especially in circumstances where one's birth family is ill-equipped to teach these kind of life lessons, you need to take "remedial classes" after you're out on your own.

In some families the lessons of self-worth and a concern for others are not learned. God created the family unit to be a safe, nurturing place for children to grow up and learn about the capacity of their own hearts to love. Unfortunately due to free will that is granted to man, NOT the fault of God, this is not always the case.

We wish to comment at this point about the tendency of people to blame God for adversity. We understand the natural human tendency to be unable to comprehend how a child could be abused and brutalized. What kind of evil can manifest in the heart of man to do this? And therein lies the answer. It is not of God; it is from the wickedness and hardness of the heart of man.

God is always there waiting, hopeful, searching the heart for the smallest scrap of change, the slightest softening but rarely is it seen until the damage is inflicted on an innocent one. And God's heart weeps also, for the pain this innocent child has to endure.

So you see that it is a complex but ultimately balanced equation. God gives man dominion over his environment, his thoughts and his will. If he chooses to create and manifest evil, that is what will be. If he chooses to go toward the light and put his energy into the fruits of the Spirit—light, peace, goodness, love and all good things—the angels rejoice.

So back to the path. Each of us incarnates with a pre-ordained mission, however the way we achieve that mission and how long it takes is up to us. Some people have to deal with a load of unfinished business before they can be free to fulfill their purpose and find their life's work. Others seem to get the idea right away and bound over the starting line with their hearts on fire with ambitions and plans.

People seem to have a difficult time with guidance and complain that they don't hear from God, so God must not be listening. The voice of Spirit is soft and subtle. Anything more would violate the treaty of free will between man and heaven. The line is open—all you have to do is pick up the phone, place it to your ear and listen.

Guidance is ongoing and constant. Guidance comes in the forms of direct speaking to you on a certain subject or in a specific circumstance and guidance also comes through synchronicity and the words of others. Have you ever had the experience of being privately troubled and agonizing over a problem in your life and suddenly your best friend will begin talking about that very thing? Or you will pick up a magazine and there is an article addressing your concerns? Heaven is not limited in its methods to get your attention. These are all alternative ways to get the message across and they fall well within the rules of respect for your free will. So do not pray to God for an answer to your dilemmas and then wait to see a plane write the answer across the sky. This will not happen! Rather learn to see guidance and synchronicity as answers to prayer and know that heaven is always listening from the next room.

Practical Wisdom: If in fact we are all born to our destiny, subject to alterations via our free will, then how do we know where to look for our life path and how do we know when we've found it? Volumes of self-help books have been written and thousands of hours have been spent in therapy seeking the answer (as if there IS a single answer,) to this question. Due to the free will covenant between heaven and humanity, we can take a pass on the opportunities that may be presented to us in any number of direct and indirect ways. Many of the most inspiring, most gifted change agents in history came to know their life path through adversity. The leaders rise up amongst the chaos to bring attention to the cause and to ignite a mass movement that can lead oppressed people out of the darkness and into the light of justice and social change. In the racist 1950s to 60s American south, the struggle against deeply imbedded social and institutional racism was ignited by a seamstress who refused to give up her seat on the bus to a white man. Rosa Parks never dreamed that her simple act of passive resistance would carve her name into American history. But it did. Some of us touch the lives of others in less direct ways but like the delicate strands of a spider's web, the vibration is recorded in the cosmic ledger.

Practical Strategy: When we are willing to hear it, guidance comes in many forms. Dream imagery is highly metaphorical, so interpreting dreams from several sources can be very accurate and lead to valuable insights and guidance.

Learn to listen to your inner voice, gut instinct, intuition, whatever you call it. Everyone on Earth is hard-wired for intuitive guidance.

Look back over your life and notice when you chose fear instead of faith/trust and what happened as a result of that choice.

Don't beat yourself up but try to recall if you felt like you should or shouldn't do something at the time, then disregarded the feeling and took the opposite choice. Saying to yourself, "I KNEW I shouldn't have trusted that person," is only half the equation. The more important part is, knowing that, why did you? The answer will probably be some version of fear.

If you feel stuck, begin to evaluate a decision from the position of "what's the worst that could happen?" When clients tell me they're "stuck" and I'm helping them move forward, I tell them to think of the worst thing that could happen if they made the choice that would move their lives forward, then consider whether they would die or not if they made that decision. It sounds harsh but it works. You might lose money, you might fail, you might look foolish, others might not like you or judge you...so what. Will you die from that? If the answer is no, then do it. The guidance in the next message confirms this.

Finding Yourself

Finding yourself has been the topic of countless books and talk show appearances. People look for answers to the normal, natural ups and downs of life, the absolutely natural ebb and flow, from "experts," gurus or the latest fad psychology, instead of looking to God. We can liken the situation to a computer chip. The chip is coded; it contains information and was programmed in such a way as to perform in a certain pre-ordained manner. You have a part inside of you that is similar in nature to this computer chip. It has pre-ordained material on it for you to access. It is part of your soul, which everyone is born with. It is the part of you that came from God and is still connected to God. God is the mainframe computer and you are connected on the network. When you are confronted with a situation that you need help to deal with—a difficult decision, pain in a relationship, health or money problems or any other consequence of living on the Earth plane—turn first within, to your inner computer program. It holds all the data you need to make an informed decision but in order to have this information be of any use, you must be willing to understand that you may not hear what you expect to hear or want to hear. You may hear that you should give up a relationship that does not honor or serve you; you may be told to leave a job that is draining your Spirit and stifling your creativity and natural talent.

At times like these it is important to remember that God's will for you is perfect. His will is always exactly what you need at the time, whether you know you need it or not. Following the guidance of the Holy Spirit cannot produce a mistake—it is impossible. This is not to say that you might be uncomfortable, or even fearful, because that is the normal human reaction to change. But if you can just summon up enough faith to transcend the immediate feelings of discomfort, sit with the guidance, roll it around in your head, get used to it and put it to the litmus test we described earlier, you will prevail. "What is the worst that could happen if I followed this guidance? And what are the chances that the worst WILL happen?" Go through the "what is the worst" exercise if you must; then go back to faith and be guided by faith in the living God when you make your decision. Listen to the subtle inner promptings of your soul voice.

Think back to other times, other places. When you listened to the voice before, did you end up doing the right thing, the best for all concerned at the time? Did you experience growth and a maturing of your higher self, your soul essence? The lessons that we are here to learn can seem harsh at times but in the larger picture—the one that God has on HIS computer screen—the harsh ripple that touched your life for a time had a higher purpose for you as well as others. That higher purpose may be revealed to you at some point in this life, or it may not. But know that you can have no finer co-pilot in this life, and indeed no finer navigator, than God.

Practical Wisdom: Some people are afraid to trust God because they think that means they'll be drafted into a life of sacrifice and deprivation. Others have been subjected to childhood criticism, rejection and abuse and have decided that they must be bad and worthless, so they feel unworthy to ask God for anything. The Biblical instruction is quite clear: "Seek FIRST the kingdom of God and all these things will be added unto you." Matthew 6:33 NIV. Here's the full passage, one that brought me great comfort and reassurance when I was in the Dark Night. Whenever the anxiety seized me, I would read the New Testament and the fear would flee.

Do Not Worry

"Therefore I tell you, do not worry about your life, what you will eat or drink; or about your body, what you will wear. Is not life more than food, and the body more than clothes? Look at the birds of the air; they do not sow or reap or store away in barns, and yet your heavenly Father feeds them. Are you not much more valuable than they? Can any one of you by worrying add a single hour to your life?

"And why do you worry about clothes? See how the flowers of the field grow. They do not labor or spin. Yet I tell you that not even Solomon in all his splendor was dressed like one of these. If that is how God clothes the grass of the field, which is here today and tomorrow is thrown into the fire, will he not much more clothe you—you of little faith? So do not worry, saying, 'What shall we eat?' or 'What shall we drink?' or 'What shall we wear?' For the pagans run after all these things, and your heavenly Father knows that you need them. But seek first his kingdom and his righteousness, and all these things will be given to you as well. Therefore do not worry about tomorrow, for tomorrow will worry about itself. Each day has enough trouble of its own." (Matthew 6:25-34 NIV)

Practical Strategy: Hundreds of clients have told me, "I don't know who I am." Some of them say, "Part of me is missing. I don't feel whole." Finding yourself is not about finding a job or a mate; it's about knowing who you are and in some cases by first deciding who you're not. Finding yourself begins with an assessment of values as well as personality traits.

Mission: Uncover Your Values

Step One: Discover Who You Are Not

Grab a notebook. Write down who you're NOT. You might have to start with what happened to you and the effect(s) it had on you. For example, your father abused you and your mother didn't protect you. Are you abusive and neglectful of others? Would you treat anyone the way your parents treated you? If the answer is no, write, "I would never intentionally harm another person." If your boss or partner was a bully who violated your boundaries, would you ever do that to someone else? No? Write that down as a value: "I am respectful, compassionate and honor the boundaries of others while protecting my own."

Step Two: Claim who you are in your heart, despite what you endured. What happened to you is NOT who you are. Remind yourself of that when traumatic memories surface.

Make two columns:

Column A: What was done to me/said to me/what I witnessed that I would never do to anyone else:

Why not?

Column B: How would I behave today in the same situations that I experienced above?

Why?

Forgiveness (see also Transitions)

Un-forgiveness is a grindstone that people they carry around their necks, from one job to the next, one relationship to the next and one lifetime to the next. Volumes have been written about the process of forgiveness: what it is, what it isn't, how to do it and why we must. Carrying emotional injuries—grudges, betrayals, judgments, any of the wounds that people inflict on each other instead of extending loving kindness—leaves scars on the mind, spirit, heart and soul. Forgiveness is the essence of freedom. It is like a warm balm that protects an open wound from infection while allowing it to heal from the inside out without leaving any trace of the original injury. What are the benefits of forgiveness? Peace, a sense of relief and a lightness in the spirit for having released a heavy burden of resentment and anger that has been weighing one down and causing a disruption in the flow of good that would otherwise flow to us unobstructed. Forgiveness is a gift—to the one who has hurt us and to ourselves. Why would we want to give a gift to one who has hurt us? By forgiving, we release ourselves to collect payment for the debt and instead sign over the IOU for karmic debt to God. We are freed from the burden of exacting repayment, which most people see as "justice" for ourselves. In ancient times and in some primitive cultures today, justice is seen as "an eye for an eye." That is man's justice, not God's. In human terms, repayment takes the form of revenge, vengeance and wanting the other party to suffer as we have suffered, or more. The higher path is for us to remove ourselves from the transaction thereby allowing the party who has wounded us to be fully accountable to God, not to us, which is a much more serious penalty.

Practical Wisdom: When we experience words or behavior from others as painful, if we have healthy self-esteem our self-love and self-acceptance is a shock absorber, enabling us to process the situation, regain our balance and connect to a loving God who always has our back. In every emotional dialogue, there's a sender and a receiver. The message can be delivered through individuals, cultural groups, religion or social media. If we perceive a comment as being critical, bullying, shaming, rejecting or as a judgment, it may or may not be so, depending on how the message is sent and how we interpret it. Let's face it—it's always easier to blame someone or something else for our reactions than take responsibility ourselves. However, when we do that, we place ourselves in the victim role and the sender as perpetrator. This is not to condone blaming the victim in cases where there's clearly a victim and one or more perpetrators, such as in a bullying scenario. But we all have filters fueled by our belief system and worldview and a mature person realizes when their buttons are being pushed, as opposed to a different reaction from someone who doesn't have those particular triggers.

Each of us struggles with self-sabotaging attitudes and behaviors. Sometimes we're able to see what the roots are if we honestly ask ourselves: "How is this serving me?" Other times we need the clear sight of a supportive friend or counselor. So when you're tempted to beat yourself up for dysfunctional behavior, have compassion for yourself instead, as you probably would for a friend going through the same raw territory. Know that the self-defeating behavior is the result of pain or fear that hasn't healed yet.

Practical Strategy: The first step in solving every problem is admitting that the problem exists. The opposite of that is an ego defense—denial. Denial blocks everything: communication, healing, progress, change and accountability. The payoff for denial is avoidance of responsibility for the problem, since when one is in denial, there IS no problem. Admitting we have a problem has nothing to do with weakness, or being unworthy or anything else. It means that we're controlled by negative, ("you won't amount to anything, you're not smart enough") controlling, (don't try that, you'll just be disappointed when you fail") or limiting beliefs ("women aren't good at math and science.") Healing and ascension means being able to address and heal those parts of us still stuck in the limitation or trauma: "Thank you for the protection. I'm grown up now and I can protect myself. You can go off-duty now, I'll handle it."

Forgiveness is simply a decision to detach from the need for "justice," which in our mind can be anything from an admission of guilt and an apology to a criminal getting the death sentence. Forgiveness is not allowing them to get away with anything because in the ordered universe of karmic cause and effect, the fact is nobody gets away with anything. The karmic leveler may not visit right away or in a manner that directly correlates with the "crime" but it does even the score. The decision to detach is difficult to make unless the emotional pain is neutralized through some form of healing. Once the charge is neutralized, that sort of puts the fire out inside us that fuels the physical, emotional or psychic tug-of-war with a person or institution. The emotional neutrality allows us to more easily put the issue into the recycle bin so it becomes something that happened to us but that no longer hurts or controls us.

God's Canvas, Living Work of Art

(Note: This message was channeled in 1999 prior to the millennium shift in 2000)

We view you as a canvas. God is the artist but you are the living work of art that together we co-create. Every life begins as a blank canvas. Your soul canvas has invisible lessons on it but the manifestation of those lessons is how your life unfolds. Just as an artist sometimes uses dark or strong colors and shapes to carry forth a dark or violent mood in a painting, sometimes life can paint dark colors over your heart. But know that this is only for a season and that you as a living work of art are constantly growing, changing and evolving. Your life is like an upward spiral of energy, reaching higher vibrations and peaks, using the lessons and wisdom gained here as a base to grow from.

Life is not without risks: physical, emotional and spiritual. But without risk, without pushing to achieve the next level, there can be no real growth. For it is only by stretching your horizons and your mind that the maturity and wisdom can take root. Just as a weightlifter must constantly add weight in order to build muscle that will take him to the next level of competition, so too must you test your own limits and push beyond them to develop your gifts and mature your soul.

The life path that we have spoken of before has been given to you in order to allow the use and improvement of your talents and natural abilities that you came here with. Many people are out of touch with and disconnected from their life path and natural talents. This is a shame and results in many false starts and unfulfilled moments. It is much better to take the time, whatever time is necessary, and uncover what it is you are truly good at. If money was not a concern and you could choose any career or calling in the world, what would it be? This is a clue to your true purpose. You will have an affinity for something, be naturally drawn to it, and it is from there that your journey should begin.

As we get closer to the millennium shift, people are turning their thoughts and hearts to spirit. There is a great spiritual curiosity and hunger in the world today. People are sick of the brutality, greed, despotism and lack of integrity that many world leaders shamelessly display. They wonder if this is going to be the status quo or is there a way for them to transcend the lower vibration of these actions and go into a higher way of thinking and behaving.

It pains us to see an entire generation polluted by the unfolding events in national politics. (Note: circa 1999.) The highest office in the land should demonstrate the highest respect and example and instead it is a modern soap opera acted out in real time. What a cast of characters! Truth is sometimes stranger than fiction. Know that at any time, you can choose to walk in the light. Imagine a spotlight following you wherever you go, and you have only to adjust your step and walk framed by the circle of light. This is what it is like when you walk in the spirit. Everything in your life, every relationship, every decision, every experience is subject to the light. You learn the art of living in the moment. Gratitude and peace become constant companions. There is no longer a need to struggle and worry because you can rest in the knowledge that your path is laid out, provisions are stored at strategic spots along the way and companions are also on the trail to help you. This is the epitome of victorious living. A knowingness that what is on the surface of life—bills and jobs and putting out the trash—are only accompaniments to life, not the essence. The essence of life is love; love first for yourself, then love for others. Love is the great equalizer. It is more powerful than hate and has the power to transmute negativity like nothing else.

So when you are tempted to worry, when you are tempted to judge, think back on the scripture in Matthew 6:25-34 (New Revised Standard Version) where it says, "Do not worry about your life... for who by worrying adds a single hour to his life?"

The greatest gift you can give yourself and the most health affirming thing you can do for yourself is to live your life in a state of grace and peace, trusting God and the angels to provide for you in every way and knowing that you are always safe in God's loving embrace.

The unspiritual mind doesn't understand karma, so they just plod blindly into pattern repeat after pattern repeat until their lives look like a roll of wallpaper or fabric, with the pattern repeating every few inches. They go through life unconscious of Spirit and the role it plays in their lives and their affairs. They do not see the obvious connections in life, in synchronicity. They do not get the idea that if you are good at something, you will probably be happy choosing it as a life vocation. It is an error to think that slavery and suffering is a necessary part of life. It is not. There are isolated incidents of sorrow, such as the death of a loved one, but this is part of the natural cycle of the universe—birth, death, opening, closure, yin, yang. There is a natural rhythm in the universe. People can pretend not to see it, pretend that it doesn't affect them, but pretending that the wind doesn't really blow doesn't make it so.

So be alert and observant, as you go through your life, for opportunities to grow. Learn to recognize them and they will usually appear as a way to interact with or serve others. Do not be concerned with money; money will come to you of its own accord. Your job is to make decisions that agree with your soul and the money will follow. So do not despair; you are part of a great adventure, this life. You need only to set your sights on something and your ship begins to turn slowly in that direction. Use your powers of imagination and manifestation to bring what you need to you. If you need healing, see yourself healthy and healed. If you need money, imagine yourself in the perfect job at the perfect salary. The universe will act upon your call and meet your needs in a very specific manner. So as the saying goes, be careful what you pray for. You might and will probably get it.

Practical Wisdom: When I was finished typing and I read back what had just come through, the beauty and wisdom of the words was stunning. I asked again for what purpose are these writings being given to me? And the answer came: to let mankind know the limitless powers of Spirit and to give hope and bring light to where there has only been pain and darkness.

Practical Strategy: Whenever you get caught up in the minor (or major) day-to-day complexities of modern life, remember that you only see one channel on the cosmic TV and God sees the entire network. Remember to exercise your faith, knowing you are one half of a sacred covenant. TRUST GOD, knowing that whatever is happening is for a reason you might not need to know right now. Take each day as it is and go on. The current mindfulness and meditation trends also help connect us to peace and to God if that's our intention, and to ground ourselves in present time. Neurological scans have shown the brain and nervous system respond favorably to meditation. And prayer is another form of meditation.

God's Spirit, The Center of the Universe

There are those who say that the sun is the center of the universe. If you look at a map of the solar system, it appears to be. But the true center of the universe is God's Spirit. His Spirit holds more energy, more brilliance and lights more lives than a thousand suns. The sun provides light but has no power to heal. It helps things grow but it cannot ignite the spark of life inside a seed. It is an element of the universe as opposed to the source. God is the power source; He is the underlying current that powers all life.

Have you ever thought how it is that the seasons change, that the birds know when to build nests (and how to build them), that the trees know when to drop their leaves and when to bloom again? All these things are due to the creative intelligence that balanced nature with man. All creatures are provided for in the food chain. Natural law is the law of the universe—cause and effect, magnetic attraction and the like.

When people try to operate out of their egos instead of within the guidelines set down by God, they get into trouble. It is impossible to defeat gravity, yet some people try to defeat other natural laws that are just as stringent as gravity. They lie and cheat and steal, then they wonder why they experience lack in their own lives. The law of karma is alive and well and operating in the world today. What you sow you shall also reap. If you plant sunflowers, sunflowers will come up, not carrots or potatoes. It is as simple as that.

So what kind of garden do you want to grow in your life? How do you wish to decorate your own soul? Start sowing the seeds of compassion for others now because there will come a time in your life when you will need the loving compassion of another. Give freely as you have been blessed so that when or if you come upon hard times or a reversal of fortune, grace will be ready for your withdrawal. Develop your God given talents and take your place in God's master plan.

You are here for a reason. Your life affects many others. It is all part of the balance. You may not be aware of these things but that doesn't mean they are not in operation around you. If someone's life is short by Earth standards, do not despair. There is a lesson in this person's life and death, for them or for someone else. It is not up to us to try to explain the mysteries of God (as if that were possible). We are here to comfort you and reassure you that you do matter, that your life does have a purpose and that there is work for you to do here. Your ripple of existence will cross and bounce off of other ripples and God's purpose will be played out for the highest good.

But what of seemingly negative events: illness, death, murder, crime? Man has been given a great and powerful gift and that is free will. He can exercise this will in whatever way he chooses and there will be a cause and effect in operation whatever he does. If he uses his gifts and energy for good, to improve life for another or for mankind, the positive karma that is created will cancel out a multitude of sins. If he chooses to move into the darkness instead of toward the light, the angels despair, for in the dark he will experience much pain and sorrow and still have the lesson to learn.

So when you are confronted with a decision/a choice, evaluate the situation in these terms. What is the cause and effect principal that is operating in this situation? The sacrifice for the good and positive action will be rewarded. When or how you may not yet know but know that heaven has taken note of your charity or your compassion and a credit has been made to your celestial ledger of grace and provision. It will be there when you need it.

In every situation, walk in the light. Turn away from greed and jealousy, for these emotions drain you of your life energy and bring nothing but heartache in return. If you need help in a situation, pray. Ask God and the angels to come into the situation and help illuminate which fork in the road is the one you are to take. Guidance is always there but you have to ask for it. State your intention and detach from the outcome. God answers every prayer but the answer may be yes, no or wait. Look for a subtle change in circumstances. Look for a softening in someone's heart or a shift in attitude. These are all answers to prayer. Don't expect a billboard or lights and sirens. The soft voice of Spirit speaks to men's hearts. And it awaits the answer patiently.

Learn to live in the present moment. As it says in scripture: "Do not worry about tomorrow, what you will eat or what you will wear. God knows that you need all these things. But seek first his kingdom and his righteousness and all these things will be given to you." (Matthew 6:33 25-34 NIV) This means live your life according to the light and you will have a lot less worry every day and fewer wrinkles on your face.

Practical Wisdom: It's important to recognize that spiritual beings (from the light, which means from God) are not allowed to predict the future, interfere with or control human will. Spiritual beings can also be from the dark side. The nature of a demon or a lesser entity from the dark side is generally negative, malevolent, intends harm and to tear down rather than build up, blasphemes God, attempts to control, abuse, causes one to do harm to self or others, urges suicide and is generally destructive. Negative entities and demons can, as scripture warns, appear to be "angels of light" but are really "wolves in sheep's clothing. Know that certain anti-psychotic and anti-depressant medications also carry "black box" warnings that these drugs can cause suicidal thoughts and other seriously harmful, mind-altering side effects.

Practical Strategy: This message directs us to give up worry about our lives. That is a difficult practice to cultivate but faith and trust are part of a spiritual practice. Start by keeping a prayer diary so you'll have a written record of prayers "sent," answers received and answers apparently not received. Sometimes we're so intent on gaining the outcome we want, that disappointment or even anger over events not working out the way we wanted keeps us from seeing a different answer. Perhaps a different answer would be a much better answer or a "no" may be meant to protect us from harm that, like a complicated series of chess moves, we're presently unable to see coming.

A client was very angry at God and felt betrayed by Him because he had prayed fervently for his marriage to stay together but his wife took up with another man and left him anyway. So why was his prayer not answered? Because God must not violate our free will. His wife's free will was to leave and he couldn't pray against that. If you look back at your life, you'll find prayers that seemed at the time to be either unanswered or that the answer was "no." If you moved ahead anyway, how well did things work out? Probably not well.

Grace

Grace is the frosting on the cake of life. It is the fuel that gets you through a difficult situation, a painful or trying time in your life. Grace is always available in abundance. The only limits are those that you place upon it yourself, through lack of faith or not asking for grace when you need it. Whenever you are in need of an extra dose of patience or understanding to ride out a situation, ask for the grace to weather the storm.

There is always enough, for the ways of spirit are without limit. Grace is a blessing that, like wisdom, is given freely to all who ask. It can give you the extra bit of time you need to think over a situation so you don't make a hasty decision that you may regret later.

Sometimes a situation needs to sit and season, like a marinated steak. Waiting and soaking tenderizes the steak. In the same way, sometimes waiting on a situation while it seasons, waiting for all the factors to emerge and seeking guidance rather than reacting in the first wave of emotion will produce quite a different result. How often have you regretted angry words spoken in the heat of the moment? How many times have you wished that you had withheld judgment, only to find out later that you didn't have all the facts and your words had wounded another? Grace is the delicate balance between contemplation and action that can spell the difference between a positive outcome and a negative one.

We all need liberal amounts of grace in our daily lives and God is glad to give it freely. It is the human condition to grapple with all sorts of complex emotions and problems involving other people that affect our lives. So when you encounter a difficult or obstinate person, pray for grace to enter the situation and the hearts and minds of all parties. Ask that the Spirit search the hearts involved, reveal any negative agendas and turn them around, coated and soothed by grace. As the saying goes, "Prayer changes things." Grace is the punctuation to prayers. Bless those around you, in your family, at your place of employment, strangers that you pass on the street. Sprinkle those around you with liberal doses of grace and watch hearts and circumstances change before your eyes. With God, nothing is impossible. Indeed, all things ARE possible.

Practical Wisdom: Grace is invoking the Holy Spirit to bring love to a person or into a situation for the highest good of all concerned. It's intending "your will, not mine be done." Grace can also be a petition for the strength and endurance to handle dark times in one's life, from illness and death to abandonment and betrayal.

Practical Strategy: Make invoking grace over people and situations an active practice. You can pray for grace for yourself or someone else when you don't know what else to do or what to pray for. Grace and wisdom are available for the asking. When you're having an attack of anxiety or doubt, when your confidence has taken a hit, ask God to cover you and the situation with grace. As the essay says, marinate it in grace and step back. Allow grace to subtly work on the person or situation to soften hearts and bring reason to a situation instead of anger, revenge or other negative motivations. Praying grace into a situation and then letting go of YOUR will for the outcome releases the power of God to flow. The results will surprise you.

A client told me about his ex-wife who was still angry over a divorce, so she took to battering him with endless legal filings for more child support even though he was paying as much as he could afford and she made more money than he did. He finally stepped back from the fight and prayed God's grace into the situation instead for the highest good of all concerned. At the next hearing, the case turned completely around in his favor, which had never happened before. The judge saw through the ex-wife's punitive motivations for the endless filings and put a stop to them. He warned her that any further filings had better be on solid legal ground or she would be paying all the attorney fees. She stopping using family court as a battering ram and they were eventually able to be civil to each other for the sake of their children. When you're tired of fighting, turn the fight over to God.

Growth, Recipe for

We want to talk tonight about growth: personal, spiritual and emotional. The process of growth can be uncomfortable but know that it is as necessary to life as food and air. If one feels unable or is unwilling to grow, this is a stifling of the spirit that is akin to death. We would like to ask a question here. What is the most frightening thing you can think of that could happen if you were to stretch your horizons and allow some growth into your life? You might discover a new talent. You might find out something new and interesting about yourself, your capacity for compassion or healing, for example. It pains us to see people who shuffle through life lockstep, a prisoner of their own fears and misconceptions about the joys and sorrows of life. They erroneously think that by staying immobile, staying constant, they can avoid heartache. Actually the opposite is true. The soul who keeps moving and growing has the greatest opportunity to attain health, happiness and peace in his or her life.

We can liken the process to trying to cook a special dish without some of the key ingredients. You'll still probably have something halfway edible but it won't taste as good or look as good as the real dish that was made with all the ingredients properly blended together. In the same way, recognize this truth. Your life is a living work of art, constantly rotating, changing and re-forming like a sculpture that is never allowed to harden. The sculptor continually makes small changes, keeping the clay moist and pliable, turning the piece on his wheel, looking at it from all sides, adding a bit here, scraping away a bit there, constantly improving and a work of art it is.

In God's eyes, you are much more a work of art than the most famous and beautiful sculpture in the world. His gentle fingers constantly mold and shape you, to delete tiny imperfections and make the whole piece a more complete and balanced work. So know that when God is "pruning" you, or editing you, it is with the greatest love, to make you stronger and more perfect and more whole than before.

Do not fear to strike out on your own, to try new things and step out into unfamiliar territory. This is the greatest opportunity for growth. There is nothing like the satisfaction and sense of accomplishment that comes when one takes on an imposing-looking mountain of a task and conquers it with grace and quiet determination. People go through a lifetime never doing this, even on a small scale. They live their lives in a sort of self-imposed minimum security prison, allowed to leave but preferring to stay, safe within the comfort zone of the status quo. They are the ones who sit on the sidelines of life and watch others play. They may never get hit by a foul ball but they'll never know the joy and exhilaration of hitting a home run either.

So, dear one, take risks in this life. Grow and change and reach out for your soul's outer limits. Do not sit home and look at life going by through the safety of the window of your glass prison. Set the example for your children. Teach them that it is good and right to challenge themselves in school, on the sports field and later on the job. Teach them that they only have to answer to themselves, their own conscience and the God within them. The opinions and judgments of others matter not at all. Some of the greatest attributes of character are developed through challenges and overcoming adversity. These qualities cannot be obtained any other way.

For example, courage. If you never confront a risk or a threat, how can you develop courage? Courage means more than standing up to a mugger. It means having the strength of conviction to say to a government or a corporation that is oppressing the poor or uneducated, "This is wrong. This has got to stop." We are not advocating social unrest or revolution here but people have been oppressing other people since time began and it would still be going on if courageous people hadn't joined together to stop it. Black people would still be in the back of the bus and unable to sit at the lunch counters without courage. Workers would still be sewing clothes in sweatshops without the courage that unionized the garment industry.

So learn to cultivate courage and a sense of righteousness in your own life. It will bring you closer to the fulfillment of your life purpose and the fulfillment of the law. Love one another, bear one another's burdens, forgive one another as the Father forgives you. Attain your spiritual and emotional adulthood and claim the true inheritance of this life.

Practical Wisdom: Growth and change are synonymous. You can't have one without the other. People fear both growth and change because it means that they have to confront something new, perhaps something unfamiliar or scary in their lives. Whether it's a new job, the first baby, a divorce or a cancer diagnosis, life is like a flowing river. When the flow is stopped, the stagnation causes the fish and plant life to decay and die. So too do our spirits stagnate when we stay "stuck" and resist the flow of growth and change in our lives.

Practical Strategy: This is going to sound extreme but sometimes extreme measures are called for. When clients come in dripping with anxiety, desperate for me to tell them how to stop change in their lives—as I was when I demanded from the astrologer to know why my life was coming apart and how to stop it—I generally tell them this: right now ask yourself, "What is the worst that can happen? If this situation comes to pass, will you die from it?" In these questions I'm addressing root chakra issues, which concern primal needs such as safety and survival. Unless whatever it is they're resisting, avoiding or fearing concerns something reckless that's likely to lead to death or dismemberment, the answer will be "NO." So if you won't die from it, what will happen? Maybe you'll be disappointed (that's survivable), you might fail (then again you might succeed), you might look foolish (so what!), other people might not like you (so what!) or whatever. But no matter what the fear-based outcome might be, you will not die from it. So address the fear, decide if it's rational, run it by someone you trust in case your judgment is too clouded with anxiety to be accurate and then do it. As long as you're reasonably sure you won't die from it, exit the confining "comfort zone." Life is too short to miss out on the adventure.

Guidance

The process of receiving guidance is frequently misunderstood. Guidance is an inner knowingness. Notice we said INNER. This means it comes from the place inside you where Spirit dwells: the God part of you. Guidance is just that; it is not a rule, it is not telling you what to do. Rather it is a quiet suggestion of a path, a choice, one that is suited to you at this point in your journey. Guidance never causes pain; it always is supportive and life affirming.

Too many people postpone joy and they live lives of drudgery and duty, rarely venturing into the playful or joyous part of life. Your common expression for this state of affairs is those who "don't stop to smell the roses." We suggest that you not only stop to smell them but that you pick a few to take home and brighten up your room and your life.

Life is not meant to be a series of painful or boring challenges to be overcome as one paddles frantically upstream against the current. If your life is presently flowing against the current, you might want to pull your canoe onto the nearest shore for a while and ask yourself why. There is no need for anyone to have to paddle upstream for their whole life. If you find yourself constantly doing this in the different areas of your life—relationships, career, health, for example—we can safely point out that you are caught in a current flowing in the opposite direction of where you want to go. You are probably navigating by an old outmoded map, perhaps the one your parents used.

The river of life is a constantly growing and changing thing. It grows new forks and tributaries imperceptibly. You must learn to read the signs and currents in all their subtlety and grace. You must learn the pattern in order to go with the flow. So choose your route through life wisely, taking into consideration all the factors an experienced yachtsman would. Is my craft seaworthy at this time? (Am I prepared to make this journey?) Do I have the rations and supplies that I will need? (Am I equipped, in whatever way is appropriate, through education, maturity or emotional healing?) Is my lifeboat and preserver in good order? (Do I have Plan B in mind if things should take an unexpected shift?) And above all, is my compass functioning properly? Your compass is your inner intuition, your built-in guidance system. It will take you safely through calm waters as well as raging storms. In life, as well as on the high seas, trust God to guide you. You only have to ask and the answer will be there.

Practical Wisdom: In my experience and that of many clients, angels or guides will intervene to protect us from danger or a life-threatening experience. Twice I've been protected from car accidents that would certainly have been fatal. Both times I was a passenger and my guides said some version of "Look out!" in time for me to alert the driver and save both of us. On another occasion in my 20s, I left an emotionally traumatized family member home alone to make a quick trip to the store. By the time I got to the end of the street, I clearly "heard" an invisible passenger urging me: "Go back! Go back! Go back now!" Annoyed, I sat at the stop sign and argued out loud with the invisible voice. "I'm only going to be gone for 15 minutes!" Again, I heard with increasing urgency, "Turn around! Go back!" So I gave in, turned around and drove a block back to the house. When I went in, the man I had left sitting in the living room three minutes before was no longer there. The bedroom door was shut. I opened it slowly and saw him sitting on the edge of the bed looking down at the handgun he was holding. I walked in, speaking quietly and calmly and without resistance, took the gun away from him. The guidance I obeyed saved his life.

When I was in my mid-40s, old enough to know better, I was on a first date with a man I met on a dating website. After talking online and by phone for about three weeks, we agreed to meet for a drink at a busy restaurant at a nearby harbor. When I saw him striding confidently toward me on the boardwalk, smiling and waving, I had an instant intuitive hit in my stomach (that famous gut feeling?) that he was dangerous. I initially disregarded the message because I didn't want to believe such a model-handsome, charming man would hurt me. About an hour later, I was forced to use a self-defense move to free my arm from his grasp as he attempted to drag me to his car. My screams in the parking lot attracted the attention of some couples who were nearby. When two of the men started toward us, I kicked off my sexy high heels and ran. Psychopath Ted Bundy, one of the most prolific serial rapist/murderers in U.S. history, was also described as handsome and charming. We'll never know if any of the women he raped and murdered ignored their survival level intuitive guidance when they crossed paths with Ted.

Practical Strategy: In terms of the body registering intuitive warning signals, most people feel that anxiety in their solar plexus, the stomach area. Intuition is running quietly under the radar all the time but unless we attune to the subtle shift in energies, we might miss the guidance signal. Learn to pay attention to how your body feels in various situations and with different people. Notice pressure, tension or any kind of negative emotion that suddenly hits you, such as anxiety or wanting to get away from someone, even if they haven't done or said anything weird. Before a word is spoken, even at a distance in an Internet chat, your energy field instantly interacts with theirs. If there's any kind of clash, you should be able to sense it if you pay attention. If there's a conflict between what your ego mind says ("but he's so handsome and charming") and what your body is telling you ("this guy is dangerous, get away from him"), obey the body first and figure out the rest later.

Health

Health is a relative term. People think they are healthy if their bodies are functioning well and according to plan. But health has other meanings as well. A pure heart, a pure mind and a clean body—inside as well as out—all contribute to a state of health. Mental health is also part of this equation. What we are talking about is a state of balance. Like the scales of justice, the moon and the stars, the planets and the seasons, life is composed of elements of balance. When something is out of balance in the world, disorder always results. When farmers attempt to grow crops and there is not enough water, the crop doesn't grow well. If they apply too much fertilizer, the crop doesn't do well either.

There are dozens of examples of balance and being out of balance in your world. So health then can be defined as the quality of the state of balance that you—in totality of all your parts: body, mind and Spirit—are in.

Taking first the health of the physical body, it is well known that certain vitamins, minerals and essential trace elements are needed to create and promote health. If there is a serious deficiency in any of these elements for very long, disease can develop. People need fresh and vital nourishing food, cleansing water and a variety of balanced nutrition for the body to be able to obtain all it needs from food.

On the mental plane, one's mind can go out of balance due to several causes. The main one is an overdose of negative thoughts, which in the extreme can cause depression or other serious emotional and mental disorders. Thoughts have energy and they have power. This is what is meant by the parable of the mustard seed. The thought and intention contained in a mustard seed-size prayer unleashes an enormous torrent of power in the spiritual realm, all out of proportion to the size of the prayer, symbolically speaking.

Jesus said, "As a man thinketh in his heart, so is he." This means that when you truly believe something, negative or positive, and receive it in your heart as truth, it burrows deep within you and begins to multiply like a virus. A negative thought seed is planted in some children such as "you're not very smart." This negative seed takes root and begins to germinate in his or her fertile subconscious. A child's mind is like freshly prepared soil. It is just waiting for seeds so the fertility of youth and faith can water those seeds and cause them to root deeply.

We have yet to see a depressed person who has not overdosed on negative thoughts, including fear thoughts. You need to learn to guard your thoughts and mind from the infection of others' negative thoughts just as you would be careful around someone who had an infectious illness. You would keep your distance and wear a mask if you had to be near that person in order to not become infected yourself.

Do not infect others with your negative thought forms and do not allow them to infect you. Keep your distance from these types of chronically negative people because their energy will drain yours like a dead battery. They have not yet learned that the life force and spirit of a person needs to be supported and infused with love, peace, humor, encouragement and hope. To do otherwise tears down, weakens and destroys the Spirit.

Many people who are in prison are there because they became infected with a fatal form of negative thinking. They do not realize that they have a disorder which landed them in prison, not necessarily that they were born with evil in their souls. Once again, as a man thinketh in his heart, so is he. (Proverbs 23:7) Criminals steal from other people because they don't know how to obtain what they need by their own power. They are using anesthetizing drugs to silence the voices that say to them: you're no good, you're stupid, worthless, you don't deserve to be loved and so on.

It is a serious error to think that people in prison cannot be rehabilitated. Some of them can. They need to be educated in the ways of the soul. They need to be told, for example, that in order to make the shift to law abiding citizen, they need to first see themselves as one. They need to mentally try this new persona on for size, stroll around in it, look at themselves in the mirror and check it out as if it was a new suit. If they can proceed past this step and they like what they see and can believe it is possible with God (for everything is possible with God), then they can be educated about how to go about transforming themselves through a renewal of their mind, which in other words is faith in action. People will, in most cases, rise up to the measure of what is expected of them. If they know they are expected to fail, they usually fail. If they know that someone has absolute faith in their abilities and resourcefulness to succeed, to conquer that mountain, somehow they find a way to do it.

Think of thoughts and intentions as roads or paths to walk. When you form the intention in your mind, and then speak it, something magical happens. Heaven sits up and takes notice, the angels are called to attention and the answer to your prayer is prepared in response. Invoking the power of heaven to help you is indeed a powerful weapon.

Practical Wisdom: This essay speaks of health and balance as a form of power. Without our health, it doesn't matter how much money we have, does it? People think money is the great equalizer. The truth is, money can come or go with a shift in the stock market. Health is actually the great equalizer. A healthy, balanced person is truly gifted. With your health as a tailwind, you can undertake the journey of 10,000 miles that starts with a single step.

Practical Strategy: Begin to notice when your mind downshifts into "negative gear." When we downshift a car transmission, we're needing to use a larger gear for an uphill climb that requires more effort and that slows us down. Then when we reach the top of the hill we just chugged up, we can upshift back into drive and take off. Negative thoughts and people are the same way. They drag us down and slow the flow of good into our lives: good health, good mood, good relationships etc. Negativity is like trying to run through water. It can be done but it's exhausting and doesn't take us very far before we get tired and quit.

Healing

In order to heal, whether it be an illness or a mental or emotional condition, three conditions need to be met. First there needs to be a conscious recognition of the problem and a desire to change it. Second there needs to be a willingness to do whatever is necessary and this may include unpleasant tasks or life decisions that need to occur in order for the healing to take place. Third there needs to be an awareness of the spiritual laws that affect manifestation and healing in the physical plane.

Healing does not always necessarily mean "cure." It can mean a natural resolution to a problem or situation, the outcome of which may not be something that you could have known or foreseen. This is why faith and a willingness to accept whatever Spirit dictates as the appropriate "prescription" is important. People often do not heal because they are unwilling to confront their fears. We find it amazing that there is such a diverse menu of fears on the Earth plane. Even fears of success or happiness—good things—provoke fear in some people. The garden variety fear involves fear of change. This is the root emotion. People continue to defy what Spirit is showing them about their health, their relationships, their job or other conditions in their life which are throwing them off balance and creating a fertile ground for illness. Remember earlier we talked about how important a sense of balance is to maintaining health.

When someone has gotten to a point where they need healing, the situation has been allowed to deteriorate for a period of time already in order for the illness to manifest. This is like a car that has not had its regular maintenance tune-ups. It will eventually break down, a part will fail and it will need repairs that are more costly and expensive than just routine maintenance would have been to keep things running smoothly. By the time illness erupts, the body is long past the time for a tune-up. Doctors treat the outward presenting symptoms but they rarely look beneath the cell tissue to discover what caused this shift into unbalanced living in the first place. A good doctor will listen to a person's physical history, then say to them, "Tell me a little about your life. Are you happy? Do you like your work? How do you spend your free time?" The answer to these questions can yield more valuable data than the most modern and sophisticated lab tests. A doctor cannot give a pill for anemia of the Spirit. Only God can fix that.

Doctors tell people not to poison their bodies. Don't smoke, don't take drugs, don't drink excessively, keep a normal weight. But they neglect to talk about the other poisons: negative and self-defeating thoughts and behaviors. For example, staying in a relationship that causes pain instead of one that nourishes and uplifts the spirits of both partners is a major drain on one's life force. Staying in a job that suppresses a person's God-given creativity and talent is another modern drain on the energy, vitality and balance needed for health and healing. With all the other stressors present in modern life today, people need to develop a spiritual practice to constantly bring themselves back into balance, whether that be a body-based intervention such as yoga or laughing with friends or walking on a beach.

So how can one restore the balance that is so necessary to healing? First one needs to be brutally honest and perhaps make a list of the things or people in their lives that bring them joy or pain. We realize that relationships are not perfect and we're not suggesting that one divorce a spouse for other than a fairy tale life. But you know when you're in a situation that is life-affirming as opposed to one where you are "unequally yoked." Do the same assessment with a job. As we stated before in the essay on how to find your life path, go back to the roots of who you are. What are your natural talents and inclinations? What are you drawn to? If you are swimming upstream you're probably in the wrong river.

Meditation is a good way for one to get in touch with some of these issues. You have to get into a place of solitude and be in an open frame of mind for Spirit to speak to you. God and the angels sense your receptivity and will never intrude until you, with sincerity of heart, invite them in. Then they will speak gently to you, bringing to your awareness those things that do not serve you, those people who are in your life for the wrong reasons and will gently guide you to rise to the occasion and claim your true inheritance as a whole, vibrant, joyful, healed person.

Practical Wisdom: Many clients over the years have shown up with what they thought was depression. As this essay points out, maybe it was "anemia of the spirit" instead. Some of them had been diagnosed and put on anti-depressants by their doctor. Clinical depression is a serious emotional illness and in some cases it can lead to suicide. In other cases, the depression people came in with transformed itself when we addressed their trauma history and/or frayed spiritual connection. Sometimes depression is found to be rooted in one of the five main emotional wounds we can experience in childhood: abandonment, betrayal, humiliation, injustice and/or rejection. A child might decide to blame God for allowing them to be hurt, when in fact it wasn't God at all, it was their parent(s.) Sometimes this spiritual damage and confusion will show up in a reading. When I bring it up to the client, some of them remember praying to God to stop an alcoholic father from beating their mother, for example, and when God didn't stop it, they decided from their child's perspective that there is no God, God doesn't love them or some version of blaming themselves or blaming God. It isn't until we heal the childhood trauma that happened to them or that they witnessed that the confusion about their relationship with God in their adult life gets sorted out. Realize that the problem is not what is "wrong" with us, it's what happened to us. Healing trauma, from wherever it is rooted in the timeline of our consciousness/spirit/soul is the key to healing and changing destructive emotional patterns that are running amok in our lives. Often physical healing results as well.

Practical Strategy: The first step in healing is self-diagnosis. When confronted with a painful emotional pattern or relationship pattern running on auto-repeat, ask yourself, "What or whom does this situation remind me of?" Chances are it will be a parent or other early experience. Once you've identified the root(s) releasing the trauma with one of the energy psychology techniques will usually bring about painless transformation. Don't attempt to treat the worst things that ever happened in your life by yourself; find a practitioner skilled in one of the energy psychology modalities who has experience treating shock, trauma and dissociation. Conventional cognitive therapies can help people gain insights and coping skills for their symptoms but they rarely release the emotional charge from a traumatic memory, or if they do, it takes many painful, re-traumatizing sessions.

Healing, Path To

There are those who believe that to find God is to find happiness or wealth or a relief of their trials and tribulations. They turn to God only in times of crisis or when they want something. They do not understand that God desires communion with us. They do not know that His love is so vast and so deep and so all encompassing, that to only seek His face in times of trouble reduces His power to "damage control."

The fullness of the Spirit is walking in the light all the time. Imagine how much easier your life would be if you never had to experience darkness, a sense of being lost in the dark. Instead your path is continually lighted by the brightest beacon, reassuring as a lighthouse beam slicing through the fog, guiding the ships so that they do not dash their bows into the rocky shoals. Life has many rocky shoals and unless you have learned to see in the darkness, you can crash into them as well. Sometimes people desire the Sugar Daddy God. They are afraid of the mature relationship that comes when you invest time, prayer and risk your own vulnerability to establish a mature relationship with Spirit.

Relationships tend to remain shallow and one-sided between people for the same reasons. If you are unwilling to risk—to show your vulnerabilities, to ask for help from your partner—you cannot truly know and love each other. In the same way, you cannot truly know God unless you are willing to trust and to put that trust in action through your prayers and your obedience. God has no desire to send you off to a life of austerity and celibacy in some monastery somewhere. If you choose that path for yourself, then that is good and that is the path for you. But most of us have paths that include spiritual communion without that level of sacrifice.

Draw near to God and He will draw nearer to you. Seek His face and He will show it to you. Open up your faith and see your life change before your eyes. For nothing is impossible, nothing is too great a task, no detail too unimportant for Him to inject His divine power into the circumstances of your life. He will never violate your free will however, so He waits to be invited. Open the door of your soul and invite Him in. Then ask for what you need and let go of the outcome. Do not limit God by deciding in advance exactly how you think your prayer should be answered.

Your mind cannot conceive of the layers of synchronicity that touch you. Like the ripples in a vast lake, you are but one tiny ripple. God knows exactly how to orchestrate the answers to prayers to bring the greatest blessings and the highest good to all parties concerned. As hard as this may be to accept, try to remember the trust and know that you only see one channel on the cosmic television. God sees the entire network.

Practical Wisdom: This essay extends a spiritual invitation into the inner sanctum of a personal, intimate relationship with the living God. Indeed it is difficult for most of us to imagine what such a journey would be like into unconditional love and the spiritual nakedness that goes along with it. The unconditional love and support of a parent(s) is only a dress rehearsal for the trust and faith we can have with God, if we consent.

Practical Strategy: So how do we enter into the spiritual communion that the essay says God so desires with us? The path is different for everyone but as we invest time and energy in important human relationships that develop trust over time, so it is with God. We have the choice to content ourselves with the cheese sandwich life we have—with its neatly folded napkin and sensible, safe and predictable glass of milk—or we can walk through the doors of a palace, where a fabulous but unknown banquet awaits. My experience with "ditch the safe, predictable cheese sandwich" and go for the unknown banquet behind door number two has been consistently good.

As scripture says in Matthew 7:9-11: "Which of you, if your son asks for bread, will give him a stone? Or if he asks for a fish, will give him a snake? If you, then, though you are evil, know how to give good gifts to your children, how much more will your Father in heaven give good gifts to those who ask Him!" (NIV, New International Version).

Hospitals

When people are ill, they sometimes end up in the hospital. The same is true for spiritual illness which can be described as a decay or drought of the soul. The spiritual hospital is within, a state that one withdraws to in order to find a reclusive state of mind and heart. Quiet contemplation, a review of life experiences and a seeking of guidance with a clear heart are the order of the day. Seek guidance when you are confused or uncertain as to the right path, how to help another person through their own trials and for your own soul growth. We understand that there is a limited amount of understanding of the ways of Spirit on your plane but this is so that through faith and trust, one can release the need to understand why things happen and to depend more on God as the writer of your destiny, your co-pilot or co-creator on this Earth.

When you enter your spiritual hospital, it might be for some quick first aid or it could be major surgery. Each person at the various stages of their life has different spiritual needs. Neither money nor social position are guarantees of a spiritual life that is victorious. The circumstances of your birth are just the beginning. It does not determine what kind of person you will become, for a strong will and well thought-out goals can defeat even the most abject poverty. Anyone who blames his or her present life on the past is deceiving themselves. Everyone starts out at the same or nearly the same start line.

Practical Wisdom: As is the case with the hospital in any city, it's always best to go there by choice rather than be carried in an ambulance. Better yet, take excellent natural care of your health so a trip to the hospital won't be necessary. When you feel out of balance, tired, sick or depressed, ask God for a spiritual diagnosis. He might suggest more self-love, more rest, some fun and laughter with friends to lighten your spirit or He may prescribe prayer to help you forgive someone who has hurt you. Don't wait until you're dying before you run to the spiritual ER—regular office visits are cheaper, faster and with help from God, the diagnosis is always accurate.

Practical Strategy: Some religious traditions teach prayers that are chanted or repeated over and over like verses of the same poem. There's nothing wrong with repeating a series of prayers but I prefer to create my own based on the situation I'm dealing with. Here's how I learned to do it. Maybe this will work for you until you find your own personal prayer style.

I first heard about the Prayer of Surrender in a *Guideposts Magazine* article in the 1980s. It concerned a mother whose daughter had a serious illness and high fever; she was dying. The mother was praying frantically for God to heal her daughter and the illness went on night after night, her daughter's life hanging in the balance. Finally it occurred to her that if God wanted her daughter with Him, she could accept that and be at peace if it happened. She could release her daughter to God and surrender to His will. Almost as soon as she changed her attitude and her prayers to reflect that surrender, a peace came over her. She walked back into the bedroom to check on her daughter and she was sleeping peacefully, her fever gone.

That story, a literal manifestation of the prayer, "Your will not mine be done," affected me deeply and deepened my faith and trust. Since then, I have seen dozens, perhaps hundreds of circumstances turn around for the best when we truly let go of our fear and need to control and turn the situation over to God and the Universe to bring about an outcome for our highest good and the highest good of all concerned. Keep in mind that when you pray the prayer of surrender, you're letting go of control and your expectation of the desired outcome. You're in effect unplugging your power supply from the wall outlet and plugging it into the electric generating plant instead. If you don't relinquish your will in the situation that you're turning over to God, that resistance—fear, lack of faith and trust, desire to control—will function as a circuit breaker and will stop the flow of power into the situation. So when you get to a point in your journey, as many people do, where you're utterly broken and on your knees with nowhere to look but up, pray the prayer of surrender; then step back and watch circumstances change. Some unconventional but acceptable versions of the prayer of surrender are: "I give up! I can't take it anymore! Do something! Get me out of this! Help me now! Thank you God!"

Karma: Unfinished Soul Business

We want to talk tonight about karma. The essence of karma is cause and effect. Karma is unfinished business. It is the essence of a soul lesson that is incomplete. We can have karma with another person or a situation in which we did not learn or complete the required lesson, so we have to keep repeating it until we get it and can then move forward. Some people get stuck in their lessons, often for an entire lifetime. They refuse to learn compassion or forgiveness or service to others, for example. But the heavens are patient and as the song says, "If you believe in forever, then life is just a one night stand." Spirit is patient and will wait until you are ready to go on.

In relationships the karma can be ongoing through several lifetimes. Some relationships are multi-themed and the threads are wound around different lessons taught by the same person. For example, you may be in a relationship where you have to learn compassion and forgiveness and perhaps love with the same person. Karma is the natural unfolding of our soul path. Through learning lessons, our soul grows wiser, more loving, more compassionate and so on. These lessons can be quite painful at times but when you walk through the fire, you come out the other side purified. Karmic lessons produce growth and strength and are necessary for your soul growth.

Practical Wisdom: In my intuitive healing work, I trace the energetic signatures of trauma in people's lives and bodies by discerning patterns of cause and effect. Then the client and I measure effectiveness by real time outcome results instead of double-blind research studies. An intuitive reading, when compared against a client's trauma timeline, gives both of us an accurate cause/effect diagnosis that often leads to profound healing. I've come to view karmic relationships as being "beyond

111

reason." Clients who are wrestling with a recurrent emotional pattern or a relationship rooted in unresolved karma will come in demanding to know "why does this keep happening to me?"

Karma is not a new age topic. Its effects are demonstrated in the Book of Genesis, the first book of the Holy Bible. When Eve disobeyed God in the Garden of Eden and ate from the Tree of the Knowledge of Good and Evil, the karmic backlash was immediate and severe for her, Adam and the serpent that deceived her. Whether the events in the Garden of Eden were actual or an allegory is a matter of belief. The point is, as Einstein said, "For each action there is an equal and opposite reaction"— OR—what goes around comes around—OR—do unto others as you want them to do unto you. We live in a world of cause and effect, aka karma.

Practical Strategy: Hammurabi's Code is an ancient system of retaliation more commonly known as "an eye for an eye." That type of revenge punishment has unleashed unimaginable bloody horror on the world for centuries and the bloodletting continues today. In the 21st century Middle East, Islamic terrorists who have perverted the teachings in the Holy Quran for their own evil agendas, are slaughtering everyone in their path and justifying it with fictional scripture. A powerful karmic backlash awaits people who torture, maim and murder in the name of God. If you're tempted to get revenge on someone who has harmed you, consider practicing restraint instead and let karma run its course. You don't get to prescribe what type of karmic backlash would be appropriate, by the way—that's called vengeance.

Love, Loss and Adventure

Love is a duty as well as a journey. Love is air, water, light and sustenance for the mind, body and spirit. People can live for a time without food but a life without love is gray and does not sustain the life of the Spirit. The game of life is an adventure of discovery of self and others— giving and taking, winning and losing, hurt and forgiveness. For without these polarities—which mimic the natural laws, including life and death—the journey to find, give and be love would hold no meaning. God, the God-force, the universal life force, is the love which holds the universe together. Even as the dark side of man—the greed, cruelty, destruction for ego's gain—breaks part of the sacred grid, love goes softly to repair and reweave hearts and minds one at a time or by the millions. The worker in the field, the purveyors of love, the aid workers and doctors, the healers and peacemakers give selflessly to repair the damage. The ones who are called to love on a larger scale—Nelson Mandela, Martin Luther King Jr. and others—change millions through their selfless example of sacrifice and allegiance to the truth that we are all one. There is no force greater and more powerful than love. For when a closed, hardened heart is opened, miracles can occur. Victims and perpetrators can forgive and be forgiven, bodies and minds can heal and profound change can be supported; for nothing is gained from the pursuit of darkness but more darkness, hate and division. But when love is injected, it begins as a flickering candle flame and can grow into a light that illuminates a thousand souls.

Practical Wisdom: Love and having an open heart go hand in hand. The open heart is receptive to others, warts and all, and is accepting while holding an attitude of non-judgment. Judgement can be defined as disapproving of others because they are different in some way than we are. Different does not equal "wrong" except in the eyes of one who judges and criticizes others. The closed heart is angry and/or hurt, wary and rejecting of others. A closed heart is a sign of a wounded heart and the "closed" sign is protective but also brings more pain because it's also closed to the offer of love. Love is an energy that flows best as a healthy river does—when the flow is unobstructed by barriers of judgment and fear.

Practical Strategy: How to open a closed heart

Inventory your own broken heart and practice love and forgiveness for yourself first. Stop judging yourself for mistakes and shortcomings. Regret is grieving over the past and the past cannot be changed, only learned from. Forgive self and others and move forward.

Practice openheartedness with yourself first, then extend that kindness to others. Be tolerant and gracious when others make mistakes. The Lord's Prayer offers this wisdom: "Forgive us this day as we forgive those who trespass against us." The prayer of Saint Francis puts it this way:

"Lord, make me an instrument of your peace. Where there is hatred, let me sow love; where there is injury, pardon; where there is doubt, faith; where there is despair, hope; where there is darkness, light; where there is sadness, joy.

O, Divine Master, grant that I may not so much seek to be consoled as to console; to be understood as to understand; to be loved as to love; For it is in giving that we receive; it is in pardoning that we are pardoned; it is in dying that we are born again to eternal life. "

Love: When Lovers Part

We wish to talk today about love. Love has a vibration and an energy that is made up of light, the same kind of light that makes up Spirit. When two people love each other or when friends or a group of people are loving towards one another, the energy of love is flowing smoothly, embracing and enveloping and nourishing all involved. Love has such a high vibration that it has the capacity to heal, even in the physical. With enough love, any situation or condition can be healed or overcome. When lovers part, they should remember the love that once bound them together. If circumstances have changed and they now find themselves with a need to move on, that doesn't negate the love that was once between them. That memory of the love should be honored and used as a tool to moderate the behavior of each partner at the time of separation. There is no need to be ugly and hurtful toward one you once loved. We find the dichotomy of this behavior absurd. This person was once the light of your life. Now that circumstances have changed, you turn your heart to stone against this person? This is an error. The Biblical instruction "love one another" is just that. It has no limits or conditions or circumstances.

Practical Wisdom: Occasionally it's necessary for me to ask for direct guidance during a session when a client gets stuck in some kind of emotional or spiritual impasse or when I need guidance as to what to do next during treatment. I tell the client, "Let's stop and ask Spirit for guidance." If they agree, we say a prayer and I start writing the spiritual dictation. The guidance below came during the middle of a session with a couple I had been working with separately and who were considering divorce:

There are many kinds of love and the deepest love is forgiveness. The power to pardon and accept the frailties and wounds of others is a powerful healing weapon. We use the word "weapon" the way a surgeon uses a laser—to pinpoint the source of disease and eliminate it without affecting the healthy tissues around it. In the same way, a relationship that has been pushed off its foundation of love, trust and safety (imagery of an ocean liner listing to one side) needs to be righted once again and shored up with renewed safety, trust and the willingness of each partner to be vulnerable and to move forward leaving the wreckage of this situation behind. One cannot survive a lethal virus if one moves out of the area of contamination yet brings the contagion along. The roots of feeling unsafe, distrustful and inability to be vulnerable need to be healed in both partners or else the venom will go on to wound the next generation.

Practical Strategy: Consider rethinking your attitudes about forgiveness—what it is, what it isn't, why you should do it and why you're not doing it. Forgiveness is not letting the party who hurt you "win." It isn't about deciding not to forgive because if you do, there won't be any evidence of what they did to you. That's an unhealthy strategy that traps you in a victim/martyr pattern. Holding a grudge to punish the other party tends to boomerang back to us in a karmic way. Perhaps you've heard the phrase to the effect that not forgiving is like drinking poison and expecting it to kill the other person. There's a difference between holding someone accountable, to require them to take responsibility for hurtful words or deeds and going on a quest for vengeance. Stalkers operate out of vengeance. Men who kill women who leave them, do it to punish their former lover for her rejection. In the Christian tradition, there's the verse from the Lord's Prayer: "Forgive us our trespasses as we forgive others who trespass against us." True forgiveness brings peace. In the chaos, cruelty and madness of today's world, peace is a nice place to be.

Manifesting

At a low point after a divorce, a client asked me to channel an answer to this question:

What do I need to change or heal in order to manifest my desires?

You have at your disposal all the information that you need to heal these fears and doubts instilled in childhood that are blocking you from obtaining the desires of your heart. What you are lacking is confidence that it can be as you decree. Your fears about being blocked from getting what you want have in a way crushed your spirit. Why try, you reason, when you won't be successful anyway? Why try to grab the brass ring when it will just be snatched away from you? You must overcome this negative thinking and negative manifestation. The universe hears every prayer, positive or negative. You must pray and meditate and be grateful for what you want. Gratitude expands and fear contracts. There is nothing you cannot have or accomplish with the powers of intention and faith trained upon them like a bullet. Write your list of descriptive goals. Then see them, feel them, BE them. And the universe will align reality to line up with and manifest in physical from, what it is you desire. In the meantime, practice being positive and your mood will follow. Keep moving toward your goals as a ship sails toward the horizon. Do not stagnate and do not stay still.

Practical Wisdom: This essay has universal appeal. Why is it that when we pray for something and invoke our faith, we sometimes don't get the result we asked for? There are dozens of scriptural references to asking God for what we need and God's faithfulness in providing. The references to releasing the fear of asking because we don't believe we'll receive and the negative thinking in that action is the central theme in this essay. When we're caught in these reversals, generally part of us is caught in the past. If Mom and Dad always said "No," when you were younger and now you're 40, why would the fact that Mom and Dad always said "No" interfere with your life now and cause you to sabotage yourself so you're still not able to get what you want? In my work, we refer to these negative fear-based beliefs and emotional patterns as "psychological reversals," which are negative, limiting beliefs, decisions or patterns that block us from healing, changing or manifesting what we desire.

Practical Strategy: So how do we eliminate these "stopper" virus programs from our internal "hard drive?" We know that energy follows thought or to put it another way, thought precedes action. So in order to manifest your desires, Jesus said to believe "in your heart" that you have already received what you asked for. Psychological reversals can be conscious or subconscious. One way to see if you have any that are blocking you from attaining a goal or healing or changing is to think about the desired outcome, then notice if you have any sense of inner resistance, anxiety, doubt or sadness about attaining the outcome. At the same time, tune in to your body and notice if your stomach tightens up for example, or there's tension or pressure anywhere else. If so, that is resistance or fear energy connected to the manifestation desire. See if any negative, limiting thoughts come to mind when you try to visualize or think about how you would feel if you attained your goal. If there is any interference, those issues--whether they be unhealed traumatic events or just negative beliefs--must be healed or cleared before you can manifest your goals or desires. The list of common reversals is in the Appendix. Apply EFT tapping on them and on the roots if you know them, until they seem neutral and you no longer sense any inner resistance when you think about them. If you can't remember a connection in your earlier life, here's an example of how to craft an appropriate EFT set-up sentence: "Even though I still have this anxiety about finding my perfect partner because part of me is afraid that what happened before will happen again, I accept myself anyway. This is just where I am right now and I choose to trust God and move forward with my life anyway."

Mysteries

The mysteries of Spirit are many. People try to understand Spirit on their own terms but this is not possible and will always lead to disappointment and disillusionment. It is like trying to receive a radio signal without the proper receiver. All you will get is static. Spirit is only mysterious because we make it that way by trying to apply third dimensional understanding to the infinite. Some people who operate out of fear instead of faith use prayers like a game of roulette. They place their money (prayers) on the red square, spin the wheel and hope that they hit the jackpot. When their number doesn't come in, they say to themselves: "See, God didn't hear me; He really doesn't care about me at all." The error behind that kind of thinking is that in order to have an answer to prayer or get God to "notice" you, you have to do something extraordinary. In fact, all you have to do is align yourself, heart, mind and spirit, with the right intention and not only will God hear you, He will answer you and move heaven and Earth to do it.

This is what is meant by the scripture that says: "If you have faith the size of a mustard seed, you can tell a mountain to go throw itself into the sea and it will do it." (Matthew 17:20, New International Version). The power of your intention and the thoughts in your heart determine what comes into your life, good or bad. The law of attraction is just as real as the law of gravity. You can't see gravity, but you know that it's there. You see its effect when you drop a glass on the floor. In the same way, faith and prayers yield results that are sometimes invisible or seem to be invisible at the time. Know that no prayer goes unheard or unanswered if it is done with the proper intention. The answer may not come right away or in the manner in which you have decided to look for it. If God played by the rules of man, He wouldn't be God!

Much heartache and pain in the hearts of men could be prevented if only people would understand the true nature of God. The universe operates by a set of laws, just like a civilized society. There is cosmic cause and effect as well as worldly consequences. When you find yourself in a state of spiritual inertia because you have created a situation through the wrong intention, take a look at the true desires of your heart and turn the situation around by turning around your attitudes. Then when you pray, with a pure heart and for the good of all concerned, you free up God's enormous power and creativity to bring healing and closure to any situation.

Practical Wisdom: This essay speaks to the mysteries of faith, prayer and co-creation in partnership with the living God. Writers and visionaries have been trying for eons to understand and explain the unseen loving, creative force we call God. The biggest mistake humans make with our limited little brains is that we try to humanize God. A powerful, loving energetic force cannot be male or female--it just is. Various religions have tried to grab authorship over God by claiming His power to be exclusively theirs. This happened to me when the nun told her class of young Catholics that the Catholic Church was the only true church. If it's true that we're all connected, that we're all one, then the many names of God should not be any more divisive than a rose by any other name smells as sweet. The workings of the human ego and its never-ending thirst for wealth, power and control that causes so much misery in the world is blamed on God.

Practical Strategy: When you have a need or an intention and you go to God in prayer, first tune in to your heart to determine if the heart has a different interpretation or motive than the ego mind. One's motivation and intention changes everything. If you find a conflict between head and heart, stop, wait and sort it out before moving forward. If the ego is taking center stage instead of the heart, you'll probably find fear, a desire to control, concerns about power, money, politics, competition, position, pride etc. A decision contaminated by these issues is not "clean" spiritually and energetically speaking and there will likely be some unanticipated fallout. If you find "contamination," you can use EFT to release them. Search your heart rather than listen to your defensive ego mind and write down what the truth in your heart says.

Pain

We've all been brought up to believe that pain is a bad thing. In reality, pain is a very good and positive thing. We know that a person born without the ability to feel pain has to be carefully watched their entire life because they could be burned, cut or injured in some way and never feel it. Some of us go through the better part of our lives the same way. We are unconscious to our own pain and that can make us unconscious to the pain of others. How we choose to deal with this pain is up to us. Some of us bury it under layers of drugs, alcohol or other anesthesia. Some of us get into destructive relationship after destructive relationship, trying to get our needs met but unknowingly sabotaging ourselves because we don't really know what it is we are seeking.

The path to conscious living is being able to see clearly where you've come from and where you're going. It means having the courage to confront the circumstances of your birth and childhood and re-write your own script according to who you really are.

And how do we determine who we really are? We look around at our lives and the circumstances and people in them and we say to ourselves, "Is this person or situation life-affirming or am I losing energy and spirit to this person or situation?" That is the litmus test. We need to be able to evaluate where we find ourselves and be willing to trust God enough to walk away or make changes as necessary in order to maintain our growth and equilibrium as we pass through the stages of our lives. What is right for us at 20 may not be what is right for us at 30 or 40. Where we came from does not have to be where we are going.

The biggest obstacle to this method of growth is fear. Fear takes on an energy of its own, and over time, can build within us like a raging forest fire, consuming us, our dreams, our plans and God-given aspirations. The only way to defeat fear is to confront it head on, look it in the face and ask yourself: What is the worst that could happen? What are the odds that the worst WILL happen? Then turn your face to heaven and pray for whatever it us you need in that moment. If you need courage to face down the fear, pray for that. If you need wisdom to sort out ego from soul, pray for that. Whatever you need will be given to you in this manner, if you only trust.

That is the journey here on the Earth plane, to learn to walk like a baby walks, one tiny step in front of the other, holding onto the fingers of Mom or Dad at first, then getting stronger and more confident, then stepping out on your own. Guidance comes from the God-within-you. That voice, which has been with you from the day you were born, is the voice that said, "Look out, don't go there" when you were in danger. It is the soft prompting that says, "You're good at drawing. I've given you the gift of being an artist or a writer or having a heart for others." Different gifts are given to all and they are there for you to develop and use to build a life of service to others.

Some of you will be teachers of truth. You have been asked to walk a path that has held pain and anguish but the rewards are also great. To those to whom much has been given, much will be asked. In these last days, the challenge will be for those of you who are conscious to be a guiding light for those around you who are not; to set the example, to live your truth quietly and confidently, showing your light as you go about a life with the fruits of the Spirit: peace, gentleness, regard for others as yourself and so on. The skeptics will look at you askance at first and may criticize your journey but eventually they will come back and want to bask in your light. They will want to be relieved of their burdens of pain and grief and unfulfilled dreams and want to know, "What is your secret? How do you manage to be so happy in the midst of this crazy mixed-up world?" And you can truly answer them: "I just trust God. I am guided by His voice within me, fueled by His Spirit, nourished by His word."

The essential truth about God is this: God is light, God is Spirit, God is wholeness and God is truth. Anything negative is not of the essence of God. We're taught by our religious leaders that rules and regulations are what matter. This speaks of control rather than the fruit of the Spirit. So whenever you find yourself judging others, engaging in gossip or causing someone else pain by your judgment, remember that you're out of your essence. You're out of touch with the Spirit of God within you. For one cannot talk from Spirit if Spirit is not in his heart.

Why are we so afraid of change? Because change represents fear and the knowledge that we must examine parts of ourselves that we would prefer remain hidden. From our earliest childhoods, we stash away into a deep dark place within us those things about ourselves that we find out all too soon bring us pain if we say them freely. We are saddled like a horse with doctrines and shoulds and after a while learn to accept that bearing these burdens is our lot in life. It is only later, when we stagger under the weight of so much doctrine and so little Spirit to balance the load that we fall to our knees and cry out to God to take this burden from us, to save us from ourselves and put us once again on the path of righteousness.

We all have free will but when we turn away in favor of our own desires, too often or for too long, we can get so far off our path that we become lost. Soon we cannot find our way back and we begin to forget how easy it was to walk in the Spirit. We become used to the pain; we become used to the disappointments and betrayals of others. This is not to say that on the path of Spirit there is no rough road. There is, but grace is there to stretch itself over the ruts in the road so that you are able to navigate more clearly, as it says in scripture: Without striking your foot against a stone." (Psalm 91, Holy Bible)

So we see that there are many paths to God. No one religion is better than another, no one doctrine without fault. The essence of

God and Spirit is timeless; it bridges the gap between cultures and languages and ages. God is light and energy, healing and hope. And we can rest in the knowledge that we are never alone.

Practical Wisdom: This essay encourages us to become aware of our pain and wound-driven motivations and to recognize how they ricochet through our lives, including their long-term effects on our health. Pain is not meant to torture, but to teach. Painful experiences have been compared to pruning a fruit tree to gain stronger branches and a more abundant harvest. So what can the pain of abandonment, betrayal, humiliation, injustice, fear, grief, rejection etc. teach us? It depends whether we close down our hearts and allow anger, vengeance and bitterness to take root, or we decide to integrate the darkness into our lives and transform it into wisdom, compassion, endurance, patience and forgiveness, for starters. As unpleasant as it is to go through, pain can also be viewed as a form of discipline. Discipline is teaching whether it's from parents or the censure of a corporate board. Teaching is meant to shift one's behavior into a more positive direction. Healing is a necessary part of growth and without it, we're the proverbial walking wounded, contaminating relationships with our baggage and subconscious drama.

Practical Strategy: If you listen closely to the way a person talks about themselves, others and their perspective on the world, you will hear whether or not they are even aware of what psychology calls the "shadow". The shadow is where our inner darkness lies dormant until we're triggered and then it erupts to do battle. You can learn to "listen between the lines" for these wound patterns when assessing a potential mate, employee, boss, friend, or just about any other relationship. If you listen to how people express themselves, you may hear the voice of the wounded child victim for example, who doesn't trust and who gets defensive even when there is no evidence of attack. Try listing the contents of your own shadow. Here's an example that a client wrote: "I don't trust others and I fear betrayal because my father cheated on my mother when I was a teenager. I can't ever let myself be that vulnerable."

Peace

Most people today do not know what it means to have peace in their lives or in their hearts. Their lives are consumed by the everyday struggles to make ends meet, to reach their goals and to have it all. They are so far out of balance that they do not know the meaning of or the benefits of peace. A balanced life naturally has times of peace in it. This is what is meant by stop and smell the roses. Many illnesses develop over time in people who drive themselves mercilessly and who push and seek and strive but yet are never truly happy.

One cannot be truly happy if one does not appreciate what one has already. Appreciation is another word for gratitude. Contentment is a valuable gift. One must develop the ability to detach from the expectations of another—including Madison Avenue—and just be grateful, or to put it another way, in a state of grace for what God has given you. Who among you can put a price on health or happiness or the chortle of a happy child?

True happiness and peace are within the reach of everyone but you have to know where to look. It is within, not in the outer material world. Even children demonstrate the transitory nature of riches to bring happiness. At Christmas, they are showered with toys and games and possessions of all sorts. Within days, if not hours, they are bored or whining about something they wanted that they didn't get or that one of their friends got something they wanted or got more than they got. When they become teenagers, it gets worse. Today's kids have a fragile sense of self-esteem and are easily corrupted by outer influences. This is due in part to the lack of spiritual training and discipline that has been denied them. They are drifting aimlessly, being swept along the flow of the latest fad or fashion. They have no inner compass to guide them so that they will not lose their way in the storms of life.

The best gift a parent can give his or her child is time and attention. Parents are deceived if they think that things can make up for the time they are giving to jobs or other interests instead of to their children. The family is supposed to be a safe haven for the child to try out his wings. He or she will go through trying on roles, various causes, interests and fads, which is part of the necessary path to development of the adult persona. Everyone has to eventually decide what they want to be when they grow up.

Parents, treat your older children like you would a friend. Be respectful of their ideas and personal space. Deal with them in as adult a manner as they can handle at the time. Create opportunities for them to learn their lessons in the ways of the world beneath the love and protection of your roof. Let them know that they are loved beyond measure, so that they will have the confidence to step out and challenge injustice and right the wrongs that they see, knowing that there is a solid base to back them up. Help them to become their fullest potential, without fear of failure, fear of success or anything other than a solid belief in their own abilities and intellect to get them where they need to go in this life. Confidence and a strong sense of self is as important as, or in some cases more important than, intellect.

Practical Wisdom: Reconsider your list of what you feel you need to be "happy." Material possessions don't bring happiness. Happiness comes from connection, love and the inner fulfillment of whatever your soul craves. When we look around the world at what people in other countries have to endure just to stay alive, we who are living in stable, prosperous democracies are indeed blessed.

Practical Strategies: Make a list, and begin with the requirements that are non-negotiable deal-breakers:--good health, proper food, a safe place to live and safe people to live with and enough money to meet basic needs. Then go to the rest of the list: creativity in whatever way that is expressed in your life, fulfilling work, a circle of interests and activities and friends to share them with. Look to the longing of your soul for the larger mission of your life here, your purpose. It doesn't have to extend internationally; it can be making the difference in the life of one person, one child or joining a group of like-minded souls who want to make a difference. Volunteer a few hours a month building houses for Habitat for Humanity, be a Big Brother or Big Sister to a foster child or find something interesting in your local community. Making a difference is very satisfying and money can't buy that. Find a way to make a difference in someone's life or embark on a path of service in your community. The benefits you'll reap will enrich your life.

Power

People think that power means money or political clout or the ability to influence large groups of people. These are all forms of power on the Earth plane but we are going to speak today of true power—personal, spiritual power. Spiritual power supersedes these other forms of Earthly power, for if one has true personal power, one can manifest all those things and the outcome will be governed by the intent with which they were manifested. True personal power is always marked by a humbleness of Spirit. Humbleness, as a rule, is sadly lacking in the world today. People get involved and seduced by the daily swirl of more and better, of besting their colleague at work instead of working as a team for the common good and all these attitudes carry over into the home.

The children who have committed the recent violence at the high schools are in search of an outer form of power because they have not been taught how to have a strong sense of personal power to fuel and guide the development of their personalities. They seek to dwell on the negative; they glorify brutal monsters like Adolph Hitler, which feeds their sickness. These children are like the lost sheep. They have departed from the safety of the flock and are wandering alone, trying to fend for themselves in a hostile and dangerous world.

We must point the finger of responsibility for some of this to the purveyors of role modeling material. The violence disguised as video games corrupt and poison a child's mind. They begin to identify themselves with the characters in violent and depraved movies, song lyrics and games. They tramp around in this mud as a form of amusement; then we wonder why they get so dirty.

The moral code of a society can be measured by how well it treats its oldest and youngest members. On this point, we are sad to say, America is failing miserably. You warehouse your elders instead of treating them as a valuable sources of wisdom and experience. Parents are busy chasing the dollar, so they don't have the time or energy to spend getting to know their children, their children's friends and really keeping their finger on the pulse of their child's life. This is a grave mistake, as your statistics on teen pregnancy, teen suicide and this rash of alarming murders at the high schools attest to. These kids are crying out for a safe haven in the midst of the assault by advertisers, moviemakers and society at large for them to grow up too soon.

The churches are strangely silent as this epidemic of violence threatens to swallow up an entire generation. Where are the spiritual leaders when these events happen? They may show up briefly in public, with platitudes and words but where is the outreach to the communities that they and their people serve? We find it ironic that the same groups who rally against abortion do or say so little as the children around them kill.

Children are like flowers; they grow toward the light. In the darkness, they can stay alive for a time but their growth is stunted and their beauty fades. These kids need to be embraced by the communities in which they live, the communities which in the not too distant future they will be running as adults. Government, churches, community groups and the public and private sectors need to band together to set the positive example.

All kids love to earn money. Create programs along the lines of the needs of each community to bring these lost sheep back into the flock. Create opportunities for them to discharge their abundant energy into positive pursuits rather than darkness and wasted hours. Set goals, motivate, provide incentives, rewards and recognition. Publicize their successes instead of their defeats. Create internships that can earn credits toward college tuition from the business community.

All these things are possible and can be created with a minimum of expense or regulation. Help these children maintain themselves before they need expensive repairs. Keep them healthy in body, mind and spirit and the next generation will survive and prosper.

Practical Wisdom: Our society and schools are in a crisis. Schools are a microcosm of society because of a misuse of power and lack of integrity from the top down. Too many politicians, religious leaders, celebrities, banks and powerful corporations are modeling the worst values this country has ever seen: corruption, lying, cheating and stealing, then denying culpability even in the face of incontrovertible evidence. Physicians are betraying the sacred Hippocratic oath, "first, do no harm," by prescribing drugs with dangerous, sometimes fatal side effects. Just because corruption is all around us doesn't mean we have to condone it or participate in it. That's the mob mentality, especially among young people, that's so prevalent in our society today, influencing everything from crowd funding to flash mobs to some obscure Facebook post "going viral" and ending up on the network news.

Practical Strategy: To guard against corruption you must have discernment. First, guard and manage your own power. Set the example for your children and those around you that you are not "for sale," in other words, that you're not one to be seduced by slick and deceptive advertising, whether it's for a "sexy" car or a political candidate with a hidden agenda backed by hidden financing. Holding your power and guarding your mind from manipulative control are equally important. You can't do one without the other, which is why the need for discernment is so crucial. So what is discernment? It's the ability to see the hidden motivations and deceptive, seductive propaganda, which underlie efforts to convince, sway, influence, control and/or deceive an individual or a group to do or not do something. If that something involves money, retention or gain of power or protection of ego, you can be sure propaganda and manipulation are involved.

Reconciliation

Reconciliation is the glue that binds up open, gaping wounds that even a surgery cannot mend. It heals up and down, inside and out, in ways that transcend language, culture and religious doctrine. It heals a betrayal between friends, lovers or countries. The energy of reconciliation is to mend, to bring peace and healing where there was once division and distrust, to bring people together in their common humanity no matter who thinks they are right and who feels wronged. It is a balm that soothes tribal conflicts that can be generations old as well as a fight on the schoolyard or a dispute between friends or neighbors. In order to have a successful reconciliation, each party has to be willing to leave their ego at the door, drop their literal or metaphorical fists and come peaceably to the table. "Let us reason" is the gentle direction. Mediation is a process whereby each party gets to put their grievances and righteous indignation on the table for all to see. Each one gets to be the injured party, demanding justice and reparations from the one they accuse of being the aggressor or trespasser. But in the light of mediation, the motives of each party are put under the spotlight. Then it becomes a matter of honor and integrity to admit that one's viewpoint of victimization and being wronged may not be so egregious after all. One can play the victim but actually be the aggressor and these motives can only be exposed by an open and honest review by an impartial judge who has no axe to grind. In the same way that King Solomon found the truth in the case of the two women each claiming the baby as their own, truth tends to rise to the surface once the ego motivations to win are swept away. The goal of reconciliation is not to win; it is to have peace and justice for all.

Practical Wisdom: Reconciliation is at the end of a long chain of actions that begin with self-examination. We have to know our own motives before we can negotiate peace with another person.

132

If our pain has not been healed, we might be driven by revenge and a desire to even the score. Nothing can be healed with a motivation to continue the hostilities rather than end them. Shouldn't I forgive, you might be thinking? Isn't forgiveness the first step? Forgiveness for most people is at the end of the reconciliation effort, not the beginning. Many people misunderstand forgiveness and what it really means. It doesn't mean allowing the other party to be not accountable; it means turning that debt of accountability over to God for collection.

Practical Strategy: The first step in the process that leads to forgiveness is healing the pain. We have to heal the damage from what they did or didn't do that hurt us. Maybe they've never acknowledged their actions and have never apologized. Maybe they're too ignorant or too full of pride to admit they were wrong. Even if we never get that acknowledgment, we still have to decide whether or not to drop our end of the rope in the energetic tug of war. One way to think of forgiveness is to allow another person to be the way they want to be, without it costing us. We have to detach from judgment, from making them wrong and just accept what is and go on with our lives. Don't make the mistake of putting your healing, happiness or life on hold waiting for someone else to "get it." You might be waiting a long time.

Relationships

In a relationship, it is important for both parties to be aware of each other as whole beings in order for the relationship to be healthy. Too many times, there is an imbalance in one or more areas that sooner or later turns the whole relationship on its side and threatens to sink it like a ship that has taken on too much water. The weight of jobs, in-laws, children and the agendas of each partner unless merged into a common philosophy, can lead to a situation of pain instead of joy and pleasure.

Too often we see people marrying for all the wrong reasons. There are dozens of them. Status, money, fear of being alone, the subconscious need to replicate a painful situation from childhood--all of these things can spell disaster for a relationship.

We wish to speak today of the essence of true love, the kind of love that is rarely spoken of in the popular culture. This love has endurance, sacrifice for the good of the union and a sincere desire for the highest good for the other person. True love is not jealous nor possessive and seeks only balance and happiness in all areas. The right person will only want the best for you and will not want you to have anything other than what brings true happiness to your heart and growth to your soul.

True love doesn't add to itself at the expense of another. It doesn't take from another to fill the emptiness in itself. This is why only whole people can make a successful marriage. There are always going to be areas of fault or weakness in the human condition and this is not what we are talking about. We are saying that one cannot expect to come to a union with less than a full and complete heart. Another person cannot fill in those empty places for you nor can money, or drugs or a nice career. If there is a deficit of Spirit, it is reflected in all of these things as well. Think of Spirit as the bottom of the pyramid. All these other parts of life are built upon this strong base and all these things are secondary to it.

When two people fall in love, they come to the table with their hearts full of expectations amid the giddiness of romantic love. Sometimes the harshness of real life is overshadowed by this romantic haze. Then one day they wake up and find that they are really not suited to each other. This is not a crime and people shouldn't blame each other if this is the case. People are born with different talents and abilities and different capacities to love. What one person may feel is the perfect kind of love for them may feel too overpowering to another.

Do not say "I love you" unless you really mean it and understand what the commitment behind those words should be. It should mean: "I want the best for you, no matter what I get for myself in the arrangement." It should mean that "I find you superior above all others." It should mean: "I give you my heart, my body and my mind so that, blended together, our two beings make a stronger and more perfect whole."

Fear has no place in love. The two cannot co-exist. They are opposites. So if you are jealous, you have fear that your beloved will leave you. The fault for this feeling resides within your own heart, not your beloved. It is something that you must heal yourself, the same with any of the negative emotions. Excessive anger, possessiveness and control all speak to inadequacies within you, not necessarily your partner. The law of attraction states that we attract that which is like us. So if you're jealous and possessive, you will tend to attract someone who is also jealous and possessive. If you trust, you will tend to attract one who is also trusting. Remember that love covers over a multitude of sins. Love has the greatest power on Earth to heal and love never fails.

Practical Wisdom: Know that the "chemistry" part of romantic attraction and how it plays out in a relationship is rooted in our family dynamics. Once again, our personal scar tissue from any of the five main emotional wounds—abandonment, betrayal, humiliation, injustice and rejection—will play out in our relationships. For example, people who suffered emotional and/or physical abandonment by a parent or parents, may abandon a partner first as a preemptive strike to protect themselves from possible abandonment. The underlying insecurities that take root in a child who is not safely attached to parents are issues of worthlessness, shame, insecurity, anxiety and for some who had it the worst, fears about survival. The survival fears don't usually manifest in fears that they will physically die but more that abandonment and loss of the parent's love imprints on a vulnerable child as a risk to safety and survival.

Practical Strategy: Nobody gets out of childhood unscathed no matter how loving, attentive and safe our parents tried to be. If you know you were subjected to one or more of the five main emotional wounds or circumstances covered in the ACE Study survey, you have some assessment and healing to do if you want to attract a healthy partner and be one yourself. If you're not sure if this universal attraction pattern has surfaced in your life, think of your past relationship struggles and see if the issues remind you of Mom, Dad or both. If they do, you'll find yourself wondering after every breakup: "Why does this keep happening to me?" If that is the case, you're stuck in a traumatic pattern that has produced negative and/or limiting beliefs about what relationships are supposed to be like. In order to heal a pattern one has to dislodge the connections between what happened to you and what you decided under the influence of trauma. For example, if you witnessed domestic violence between your parents, you may have decided "men can't be trusted, men hurt women," or "love equals abuse; I'll never trust again."

Religion

Religion vs. Spirit: what is it? We can liken the difference between religion and Spirit to traffic laws. When the light is red you stop, when it's green, you go. In this way, everyone knows how to avoid a crash and everything usually moves pretty smoothly. And each and every time, if someone decides to test the waters and see if in fact running a red light in the middle of heavy traffic will produce a crash, they are generally not disappointed.

In the same way, organized religion sometimes produces people who blindly follow the rules because they have been taught that to not follow the rules will produce a certain spiritual crash. The dogma that pervades most organized religions in the world today is not for the glory of God but to control and manage the flock so the shepherds have an easier time. It's easier to manage a large flock of docile, not-very-bright sheep, than it is a herd of spirited, independent-minded, wild horses.

Religion, rather than bringing the fullness of the Spirit into the people, as God intended, tends to wring the Spirit right out of them. They become like blinded docile sheep, blissfully following along, never having to grow or think or own for themselves what challenges and lessons God might have otherwise had for them. They stay protected (they think), spiritually speaking, inside the circled wagons of their chosen sect, believing their tribe to be the only righteous ones, the only saved ones, the only ones that God has chosen to grace with His Spirit.

In reality these people are blind to the fullness of true Spirit and wouldn't know the voice of God if it shouted at them in the shower. We find it curious that man's need for protection and safety and the abhorrence of any kind of change is so threatening. We see the majority of those who call themselves spiritual trudging through life in lockstep with the others in their church or synagogue, behaving themselves, playing by the rules and suffering a drought of the soul the likes of which have not been since the time of Christ.

Spiritual hunger today is an epidemic. The hungry need to be fed and the thirsty given spiritual water. As scripture says regarding man's quest for the comforts of the physical body, food, clothing and the like: "God knows that you need these things. But seek first his kingdom and his righteousness, and all this will be added unto you." Matthew 6:33 NIV.

This means that God wants you to put Him first in your life. Your spiritual life is just as important as your physical one but since it is subtle it is easily ignored and drowned out by the hustle and bustle of this world. Spiritual malnourishment can be prevented with a few simple rules:

1) Never go to bed hungry. That is to say, without partaking of the fruits of the Spirit sometime during your day. The fruits of the spirit are love, joy, peace, forbearance, kindness, goodness, faithfulness, gentleness and self-control.

2) Confess your sins and shortcomings to God, who forgives and strengthens all who ask him. There is no need to make a public spectacle of your sins; this is a matter between you and God. The sacrament of confession means in love and support, bear each other's burden of sin and offer each other comfort and forgiveness. It does not mean form a tribunal and drag people in front of it to publicly humiliate them.

3) Read the sacred texts, for this is where you will hear the voice of God.

4) Pray unceasingly knowing that no request is too small or no mountain too big to be thrown into the sea by the mustard seed of

faith. Then sit back in peace and wait for the answer, knowing that with God, all things are possible.

Practical Wisdom: Most people are brought up in a religious tradition that is handed down from their family ancestry. Some also go to religious schools and colleges, further grounding them into a particular religious belief system that is frequently dogmatic, rigid and excludes other perceptions of God. As a result, we become judgmental of other interpretations of God which can cause us to confuse "our truth" with "THE TRUTH." One example of THE TRUTH is gravity. It always works, no matter where, when or who is putting it to the test. Gravity always wins. The same with the universal laws of God, many of which can be found in all the Holy books, such as do not murder or do not steal. The downside of religious exclusivity is that dogma and man-made rules and regulations can supersede a one-to-one connection to God.

Practical Strategy: Belong to whatever church, political party, social group, conservation movement, animal protection society or other cause that you like but don't allow your individual identity and personal power to be absorbed into the group identity.

This is harder than it sounds. You'll know this is happening when you are subtly manipulated or overtly pressured by the group to compromise your beliefs or integrity or to sacrifice some aspect of yourself in favor of the group agenda. Members of the military do this because their service requires them to supersede individual moral tenets against killing in order to carry out their mission and maintain the order, discipline and unit cohesion that's necessary for the unit's survival in combat. Think carefully about what your membership in any group will cost you in terms of your individual identity, expression, self-sacrifice and power. In the case of religion, assess whether membership in the group serves you if it requires you to sacrifice connecting to God in your own way and on your own terms.

Rwanda

(This short channeling was hand written on a scrap of paper in the summer of 2004 at a restaurant after seeing the movie "Hotel Rwanda." The graphic scenes of cruelty and genocide depicted in that film that are happening on a more global scale today, left me shaken, so I asked for guidance and this is what came.)

We are all connected. We are all one. The God presence inside us is the same. We are all born of the same seed. As we do to each other we do to ourselves and those we love. It is a sin of the highest order to ignore the suffering of your neighbor, even across the globe. This is what is meant by the brotherhood of man. We are all seeds of the soul of the same God.

School Shooting

(After the Columbine High School shooting, I was affected for weeks by the senseless violence unleashed by two teenage boys on their helpless classmates. Once again I asked for guidance. At the time, I thought the reference to drugs was about street drugs the boys may have taken. It has subsequently been revealed that at least one of them was on prescription psychotropic drugs that may have increased the propensity toward homicide and suicide, which we have seen repeatedly in the combat veteran population and other mass shooters.)

You asked us earlier about the school violence. Once again, free will coupled with the forces of darkness on young and easily misled minds are at the root of this destruction. Drugs have the ability to alter minds in more ways that just the elements of the chemical substance. Drugs scramble the picture on the cosmic TV. They distort and pervert the self-image, so that the more drugs are taken, the more the person comes to depend on them. They bring pain and anguish rather than the escape and dullness of reality that most drug users are seeking. The kind of peace they are seeking cannot be found in a chemical substance. They are suffering from anemia of the soul. It is a long road back for these children but they can be reached and they are worth saving. They are off the track, like a train. Their forward travel and growth has been shunted off to one side, where it stops until they are placed back on the track once again. Your purpose here is important. One person can affect the lives of many.

Self, Prayer and Faith

The notion of self can sometimes be a puzzling one. The self, or the Spirit as we prefer to think of it, is an integral part of the soul and is the bridge to the physical body. The soul has the imprint of life lessons inscribed on it and it is the job of the self to carry these lessons out for the good of the person who is here to learn and grow from them.

Lessons come in many forms. They can be taught by other people, both in a positive or negative context. On the positive side, we learn to love by giving and receiving love. On the negative side, we learn to forgive after we've tasted from the bitter cup of betrayal and pain inflicted by one that we once loved or trusted. Eventually one comes to a point where healing must begin in order for growth to take place and lessons to be learned. The free will that God allows us on this plane can be directed and used to advance or hinder our progress.

Many times, Spirit tries to get our attention to make changes in our lives, to move us to even greater heights of accomplishment, service to others and love of ourselves. For it is always from a place of love that true growth begins and flourishes. Love is the healing balm of this life. As it says in 1st Corinthians 13:7 (NIV): "Love always hopes, always protects, love never fails."

Your journey here is a play with many acts and the underlying theme is love. To love is the highest vibration; it is the highest calling. People need love as much if not more than they need air, water and food. If you are acting from the heart, from a place of love, you will not make the mistakes that you would if you were reacting from the ego mind. The ego mind speaks a different language. It speaks of self-gratification first, the never ending search for more and better things, the illusory "security" that people think money can buy, when in reality, the only true security is from Source, from Spirit, from God.

Your thoughts, to the extent that they are in alignment with Spirit, determine your health and your security. If you dwell on thoughts of fear and discouragement, don't expect your circumstances to take a positive spin anytime soon. You are putting forth your "order" and what you ordered is what you will receive. Think of it as ordering from an Internet store. You look at the pictures and a description of the item, you place the order with a point and click, you accept that the order will be processed and arrive as specified, then you sit back confidently and wait for the UPS man to appear at your door. You don't spend hours worrying about it, you just accept that it is done. It is a process and it works every time.

So why is it that people have so much trouble with spiritual laws and universal principals? It's not any different from where we sit. The desire for the item is the need that you have which you want to pray about. You plant the seed by thinking of the answer you would like and then you speak it, which is like placing the order. You submit the order and wait confidently for the answer to arrive. This is how spiritual growth works. And every time your order is delivered in good shape and on time, your faith grows and your spiritual power grows. When you pray, Jesus said, believe that you have received what it is you ask for and it shall be done for you in heaven. It was true the day he said it some 2,000 years ago and it's still true today. "Jesus Christ is the same yesterday and today and forever." says in Hebrews (13:8 NIV). God won't change the rules on you in midstream. He can't, for to do so would be to deny his own omnipotence and upset the order of the universe. So when we talk about spiritual truth, we are talking about timeless facts, incontrovertible truths and the dependability that comes when the sun rises in the Eastern sky.

When parents are raising their children, they should always remember that their children's minds are like blank slates. It is an awesome responsibility to be a parent, to have the duty to bring up a child to be kind, unselfish, considerate of others, yet have the self-esteem, the strong sense of self, to withstand the many storms that life will bring to him or her. Parents, equip your children with emergency gear to survive life's emergencies and unexpected storms as you would prepare for a long hiking or camping trip. You'll need rain gear, for the inevitable rain that falls in each life. You'll need flashlights to illuminate the darkness that comes as surely as the light also does. They should also be equipped with wisdom to think for themselves and to reason, using their inner guidance to solve problems. A child that is equipped with these basic tools can overcome any obstacle and go on to be happy and successful. When God gave us brains, he also added intuition, self-reliance, confidence, persistence and faith in oneself as well as in God. Many of this century's most impressive entrepreneurs started with nothing and came from poor families. The lack of wealth in your family of origin is not an excuse for failure to achieve your own dreams. You were born with everything you need already inside you. God gave you brains, intuition, an innate sense of right and wrong and an indestructible Spirit.

So remember, in this fast paced Internet world, the old rules still apply. When you are hungry, eat. When you are tired, sleep. When you are in trouble, pray. When you are happy, pray. When you can sit down and reflect on all your many blessings and joys that have nothing to do with money, thank God for His provision and his faithfulness.

Practical Wisdom: One of my clients came in practically paralyzed with fear of the future. She was afraid of cancer, terrorism, losing her job, her husband losing his job and a list of other fears that would keep anyone up at night. For a while I listened to her spiral herself into near hysteria; then I leaned forward and said to her point blank: "Listen to me. Security is an illusion. You're a heartbeat away from being a widow, a car wreck away from paralysis, a cancer diagnosis away from pain or death, a stock market crash away from financial ruin, a September 11th away from terrorism. Stop obsessing about security because there is none. Control and security are big illusions and I'm popping them like a balloon right now. There is only faith. "

She stared at me, speechless and then after a moment said, "I guess you're right. Anything can happen in the blink of an eye, can't it."

Practical Strategy: The need for discernment is constant. Discernment is going inside your heart center, not your mind, and asking yourself in complete honesty, putting aside any fears or self-serving agendas you may have:

- "Is this right for me?"

- "Does it FEEL right?"

- "Is the TIMING right?"

- "Does this job or relationship feel really, really right in my heart (or gut)?"

If there's any sense of inner resistance, note it, attempt to clear it with EFT or another healing method in case it's just old fear programming interfering, and then take another look. If the peace, contentment, the "knowingness" that this is right and meant to be for you is still not there, then your inner guidance is trying to tell you either "no" or "wait." Something is not right. Inner guidance is that whispery "gut feeling" intuitive voice inside of us. Everyone has hunches but there's an art to listening to them and acting on this guidance. This is where the term "counter-intuitive" comes in. Intuition is subtle and unless survival is at stake, it won't fight our ego for air time. Rather, we need to cultivate it and invite it to be present with us.

Seven Deadly Sins

From the perspective of heaven, the seven deadly sins are not really so deadly. It's all in how you look at what the heart's intention is. Greed has negative connotations and with good reason. Greed means one's relationship to the power of money is out of balance. Whereas scripture talks about abundance and the blessings of heaven poured out into your lap measured and pressed down and shaken together, greed is the perversion of abundance. Greed springs from insecurity, the kind that means there is a deep hole in the personality, a nagging insecurity that can never be filled with mere money. The cause of that insecurity is a spiritual hunger; a desire to know God and to relax in the knowledge that lack is not a normal condition. There is enough for everyone. If your life is in balance and you're using your talents in the way God intended, you will always have everything you need.

Those who are killing themselves with work to the exclusion of a healthy family life, fun, rest and creativity will recognize themselves here. The nagging in the soul that says more, more and more cannot be quieted by more. That longing can only be satiated by Spirit and knowing that with God, there is always enough.

The next issue we would like to discuss is theft. Theft is a cousin to greed, in that taking what does not belong to you is again rooted in low self-esteem or an unhealthy self image. It is a spiritual error to rationalize your taking something because you lack it and need or want it. Perhaps you are being placed in that temporarily needy circumstance to learn compassion for others or to really appreciate what it is that you do have.

When viewed on the cosmic scale, these human concerns that people spend so much time fighting and fretting about don't amount to a hill of beans. Our concerns should be on a much more global scale. What is the reason for all the killing, the "ethnic cleansing" currently going on in various parts of the world? The divisions between the races is another big issue. Think for a moment the progress that could be made, the jagged tears in the heart of humanity that could be mended, the children who would grow up learning to love instead of hate, if people could see past skin color to each other's hearts.

The true essence of man is buried under layers of media hype and commercially created "happiness." What do you need to be happy and powerful according to Wall Street and Madison Avenue? A new car every year, a ton of money in the bank, not to be used for the good of anyone but yourself, not to be donated to the poor or used to alleviate anyone's suffering, but to stay put and earn interest...to have Bigger and Better and MORE—in Everything.

We sit back and watch the incredible waste of time, energy and talent on accumulating all these things, things that as scripture teaches could disappear in the blink of an eye. "Do not store up for yourselves treasures on Earth, where moth and rust destroy, and where thieves break in and steal..." (Matthew 6:19-21 NIV).

Even more disappointing than the accumulation of so much "stuff" is the accompanying attitude. There are people on this Earth who have amassed enormous fortunes, more money than they could ever spend if all they did was spend money until the day they died. This money, which in your terms represents enormous power, is not being used; it is being saved so that people can maintain their standing on the *Forbes* Annual Report list. The women who are being beaten by their drug and alcohol abusing husbands, the children who are moved furtively from one homeless shelter to the next lest the law get wind of them and take them away from their poor mothers, the diseases that could be cured—we could go on and on.

But this is the human condition. God allows these circumstances to give men the opportunity to take the high road—to make the independent choice to rise above the crowd of popular thinking of the time and make a difference.

If one high-profile millionaire in the manner of Ted Turner, who recently set such an example, started a foundation to address these needs and begin to right some wrongs, the blessings of heaven would flow like the Nile to support his or her cause. People would be motivated to help, galvanized into action to take up the same spirit and real progress could be made.

Oprah Winfrey is such a soul. She has a higher consciousness and a heart of compassion born out of her own pain and struggle with adversity. She uses her talent and influence to turn people's lives and hearts around, one by one if necessary. It is no small accident that not only is she blessed financially beyond her wildest dreams but she has the respect and admiration of millions of people. Her word can make or break a cause or a person. That is what we mean by using your talents wisely and affirming that God is really in your heart.

Practical Wisdom: Working for God doesn't necessitate accepting a vow of poverty and a lifetime of sacrifice. It means that when you align yourself with your life purpose, which is why you in all your individuality is on this planet, you are signing up for important work in God's larger plan. In the essay "Self, Prayer and Faith" it says faith is trusting without any doubt that the item you ordered online is on its way to you and not to worry about when it will arrive. The seven deadly sins refer to the excesses that fear drives us to when we're insecure and yield to fear and worry about what we don't have instead of offering gratitude for what we do have. Again, it all comes back to power and how we manage it. If we feel the need to cave in to greed and/or theft, we're telling the universe that we do not want the banquet waiting for us and prefer the cheese sandwich we have in our hand. When adversity unwound life as I knew it in the space of a few weeks and I was in a panic, a wise teacher calmly said to me, "I smell God." She was right. A path of service to others is always a high spiritual calling and when you're working for the light, your needs will always be met.

Practical Strategy: One person with drive and passion can make a difference in this world. Even children have raised money to dig wells in Africa so the people don't have to walk miles for clean water. Decide to follow the path that presents itself to you. It might be something you read, or see on TV or the Internet or some "chance" encounter. If there's a sense of animation, a spark of interest, a feeling inside that this is something you need to do or support, then do it. It doesn't matter if that's the path you'll end up on; it's the path for now. It also doesn't matter where you start; you'll eventually wind up on the path you're supposed to be on. Inventory your natural talents and gifts, decide which social issue or injustice or cause speaks to your heart, then take the first step and let God handle the rest.

Sin

We wish to discuss what constitutes sin. People think that sin is an offense against God and the Holy Spirit and in a way it is. But the deeper reality is that sin is an offense against the human Spirit. The sins that are listed in the Ten Commandments for example, are sins against one's fellow man. Do not murder, do not steal, do not covet another man's wife, all speak to the evil that man is capable of storing up in his heart. These sins are sins against his fellow man and not only against God's law.

With free will thrown into the equation, man is really in a quandary. He knows what God's laws are and the penalties physically and spiritually for violating them. But at the same time, he betrays himself and his soul by behaving in an incongruent manner. The scripture that says, "Which of you, if his son asks for bread will give him a stone," illustrates this dilemma. (Matthew 7:9 NIV). With free will operating, a man has the ability to choose to act in a manner that depicts evil or good. If he chooses evil, he sins first against himself, then against his fellow man, then against God. This is how Karma is created. There's an energetic debt to be paid when one commits acts of evil or dishonesty and a Karmic accounting of grace and good to draw upon later if one does good. When Jesus said, "It is easier for a camel to go through the eye of a needle than for someone who is rich to enter the Kingdom of God" (Matthew 19:24 NIV), he was commenting on how riches, if not handled by a spiritually mature person, can corrupt and complicate a person's life to the point where "love of money is the root of all kinds of evil." (1 Timothy, 6:10 NIV).

We wish to state that money is not bad and having less of it than the next person does not make you more holy than your neighbor. Conversely money can be a great equalizer and can elevate the downtrodden. Money is only a cosmic tool that can be used like intellect, aptitude, talent or beauty to shape the world in which you live. Money, in and of itself, has no bad or good connotations. It is the hearts of people who are corrupted by the dark side of what money can bring to a life that are evil. As we mentioned earlier, in the cases of Ted Turner and Oprah Winfrey, money can be used for a powerful good. And so can a gun. It can be used to protect innocent life or destroy it. Think of this the next time you are tempted to use money to corrupt yourself or another or to attempt to influence events in your favor by "buying" something or someone.

Practical Wisdom: "Sin is an offense against the human spirit." That's a novel explanation, isn't it? This concept is affirmed by the "trespass" reference in the Lord's Prayer. "Give us this day our daily bread, and forgive us our trespasses as we forgive those who trespass against us..." This guidance reminds us to be congruent and in alignment with spiritual principles and to resist sin which is breaking spiritual law, resulting in damage to ourselves and others. When an investigation is begun into wrongdoing at the local, corporate, government or international level, people say, "Follow the money." Love of money has been elevated to the worship of a false god in this country and this world and we are witnesses to the death and destruction caused by it.

Practical Strategy: Decide for yourself what your personal monetary policy is. Use money to contribute to good works by others or create good works and a www.gofundme.com campaign to fund it yourself. Engage spiritual law, the law of Karma when you are temporarily running on empty. Tithe, perform acts of service and see what good comes back to you, multiplied.

Spiritual Groundbreakers

We want to talk tonight about horse racing. In a horse race, the various pedigrees are matched against one another in terms of age, recent wins and abilities in the stretch. In order to make the race interesting, there has to be a mix of horses. There has to be some long shots, some middle ability horses and a few that could win. Then when the bets are placed, there's some excitement and competition.

In the same way, we want to express that people can also be nags or thoroughbreds. It all depends on pedigrees, training and a certain undefinable spirit that the horse or person is born with. If someone has a lot of spirit, their tenaciousness and drive to win can make up for a lot of disadvantages in their background, upbringing or pedigree. In some cases of some very famous and accomplished people, the drive or spirit is all they had or makes up most of what they had to work with. They may have had little or no education, come from a poor family and had no role models who broke the ground for them.

Spiritual groundbreakers are those people who are called by Spirit out of whatever career, lifestyle or pursuit they happen to be in at the time. They hear the call, heed it and step forward in faith, knowing that God will provide the education and pedigree. These are some of our most powerful teachers, leaders and healers because they stepped forward in faith and had to depend on God to show them the way.

Know that when you are called, you are being called into God's perfect will for you. Nothing you could possibly dream up or pursue out of your own power could possibly bring you as much satisfaction, joy, growth and opportunity to serve as being in God's will and walking in his light. "The eye has not seen and the mind not conceived what I have prepared for you," Jesus said. At the time, he was talking about heaven but he also meant heaven on Earth, in a state of grace in which one is literally creating heaven on Earth through service and alignment with God's perfect energy and will.

There can be no greater satisfaction of productivity than when one is being directed by the one who created you and wrote the directions for how to operate you. Who can know better what is best for you and your higher purpose than the mind of God?

So from now on, exercise your free will to make the best choice in your life path. Start with what it is you are good at or have an attraction for, whether it is underwater photography or elephant training. The world needs all of that and more. Know that God wants to co-create a perfect heaven on Earth with you and for you but He needs your permission. Step out and seek His guidance and you will be guided. It will have a certain right or familiar feel to it because you will be tuning in to the frequency of the seed that has already been planted within you: the seed of your own potential. You will need to identify it, then work with it to develop it into its fullest potential. You will be guided along the journey and people, books, classes—all the tools you need to reach your goal will come to you. They cannot NOT come to you if you are in God's perfect will. He will see to it that you have everything you need in order to fulfill your contract. You may not know how or when this is going to happen but you don't need to. That is what faith is all about. If God revealed his plans in advance, there would be no need for your faith.

So reach for the stars, dear ones. Expand your minds and dare to dream, for your dreams have power and they turn into desires and intentions, which are prayers that have caught fire. They are urgent demands for assistance from heaven and they will be answered. Then you and God can move forward in grace and confidence, fulfilling your contract with life and being the pebble that starts a ripple in a clear, mirror-finish lake spreading outward and touching lives all around you, in ways large and small. Acknowledge the source. Plug your power cord into the most powerful outlet and watch the power flow. It will light up your life and power up your dreams beyond your own imagination.

Practical Wisdom: Throughout the ages, people have agonized over the answer to the topics addressed in this essay and the one titled "Called." What deeper, more life-altering existential questions are there than "What is the purpose for my life? Why does it matter that I am here?" The essay clearly directs us to take action by exercising our free will in alignment with God's perfect will for us. This is a co-creative partnership decision, not one that is imposed on us. Free will is just that—God ignites the spark of divine potential that we incarnated with, which is the seed of development of our personal potential and calling or mission. Tragedy, adversity, illness or betrayal can form the framework that dismantles our dependence on people and forces us to look instead to God. When we agree to accept the contract and to move forward in faith, every step is covered by grace, even if we can't see it at the time.

Practical Strategy: Everyone is gifted in some way. Gifting doesn't always show up as an ability, like art or teaching. It can also be a spiritual quality such as faith, prayer or healing, or an attribute of the heart: love, empathy, compassion, forgiveness. What are you good at? What brings you inner peace and fulfills your creative urges and the desire to make a difference? What do others say you're good at? Start there. If money or geography was of no concern, what would you be doing with your life that might benefit one person or ignite change in the world?

Spiritual Malnourishment

There are those of you who are seeking to have a greater balance in your lives. You feel a certain sense of disconnectedness, a lack of joy and excitement in your daily lives. You go to work, attend to the needs of your families, shop and cook and function in your outer world but you still feel an emptiness, a sense of "what else is there for me?" We wish to talk today about this sense of spiritual malnourishment, a kind of spiritual lack.

People who blindly follow their daily paths are not cognizant sometimes of what else life is really all about. They see things in a one-dimensional manner in the physical: food, clothing, money etc. We want to take you into the deeper underlying levels of what this life is meant to be and what is there for you if only you are willing to open your eyes and see.

You are here for a reason: to do a chosen work that will affect your life as well as the lives of others. When you are in touch with this concept, you begin to look for meaning and purpose and synchronicity, where ordinarily you would not see any. Your purpose is not necessarily your job. It is much bigger than that. It is the essence of what we are all here to learn: first, to love, then to forgive and also to find happiness, growth and satisfaction in service to others.

If you never give from the heart, with no thought of what you will receive in return, you will never know the exquisite joy and pleasure that act brings to the giver. Many people go through their entire lives never once being able to free themselves from the curse of materialism. They are like hamsters on a treadmill, running and chasing but never finding what they want most.

What people actually want most but which most are not in touch with is peace. They think that if they accumulate every material thing, they will be happy and that is what peace is. This is a major error. Happiness in the way that you on the Earth plane think of it does not necessarily bring that most precious commodity, peace.

Peace can be defined as contentment with the present, living in the moment, not worrying or planning or scheming for the next day or the next week or the next year. It is a Biblical peace, the peace that surpasses all (human) understanding. This kind of peace comes at a price for most people. It can mean the end of a relationship or perhaps a draining job and usually results in a redefinition of the self.

Many people are extremely reluctant to go this deeply into themselves in order to discover and reach this place, this state of being, this level of grace because they are too afraid of change. But peace is well worth the price and time and introspection involved.

Can you even imagine how much your life would change and how much more energy you would have for creative pursuits or service to others if you were so confident that God had your life well in hand and that provisions that you are not even aware of are being made ready for you? Then you would have this peace that surpasses all understanding. It is not really possible on the physical plane to achieve this kind of peace and freedom from worry without faith and without actively seeking God's grace. But when you do, you will find that you have discovered a rare and precious thing. You will have plugged into an enormously powerful yet gentle source of power and provision. For what can be better than having the living God as your anchor?

Practical Wisdom: The essence of this essay is what modern psychology calls "mindfulness," which is keeping one's thoughts and consciousness in present time as much as possible. For those of us who have survived a significant amount of childhood trauma, myself included, mindfulness means present time is the safety zone. Being grounded in present time is a tool to protect ourselves from being trapped in an automatic re-run of the past or to scare ourselves with thoughts of a desperate future that is not real because it hasn't arrived yet and in fact may never arrive. In cases of severe trauma and PTSD, intrusive thoughts and flashbacks can take us over temporarily and we have little control over them until the traumas that are causing them are healed. With consistent practice, the protective shield of present time allows us to look back at the past as if it was an old photo album, without becoming trapped in it. We can then close the memory album, put it back up on the dusty shelf and return to the safety of present time. Since present time protects us from being held hostage by the traumatic past, there's no further need for addictive "anesthesia," dissociation, avoidance, projection of our pain onto others, self-sabotage or any of the other ego defenses that hurt us and hurt others. It means that when we firmly ground ourselves in the safety zone of present time, the future is a blank slate awaiting our creation. It means that in present time, WE are in control.

Practical Strategy: When you find yourself moving backwards in consciousness, feeling regret, shame, guilt or beating yourself up for something you did or didn't do, come back to present time and open your self-treatment toolbox. Treat the memory with EFT or TAT which will rebalance your energy and bring another part of your spirit into the safety of present time and help you to forgive yourself, forgive others and move forward.

Structure of the Universe, Cause and Effect

We wish to talk tonight about the structure of the universe. The universe is made up of planets and solar systems but it is much more than that. What we are going to talk about cannot be measured with scientific instruments; it can only be felt in the human heart and soul.

The universe is indeed one of cause and effect, as Gary Zukav says in his fine book. We want people to know that they have enormous power to create change, positive or negative, in their lives and the lives of others with their thoughts. As a skilled architect creates the blueprint on paper that will later become a solid building made of steel and wood and concrete, so too do your thoughts create solid reality in your lives.

When you are operating at this level of power, you are creating as the universe was created, out of thought energy. You are using the currency of Spirit. As it says in the Bible, "...and God created the heavens and the Earth;" in your terms understand, he "thought" it into existence. You will recall the parable of the mustard seed. On a practical, Earthly level of reality, it would seem quite impossible for a person to say to a mountain, "go and throw yourself into the sea" (Matthew 21:21 NIV) and rationally expect that event to occur. But in the spirit realm, where there is no time or space as you know it, this is not a difficult task.

In healing, the energy of the physical body or condition has to be addressed in spiritual terms. One has to look at the person and say, "What thoughts of yours contributed to the creation of this illness?" The person may be quite unaware that they had anything to do with creating the illness and in some cases, such as with genetic and environmental causes, it's true, they didn't have anything to do with it. But in many cases, people's negative thoughts do come together over time and gather enough power to cause illness, like a wave that gathers shape and speed as it forms, then breaks on the beach.

Every work of art, every painting, sculpture, movie or any other type of creative endeavor starts with the thought or conception of an idea. To the extent that the artist puts energy and motion into the original thought, the idea begins to evolve, take shape and slowly mature, like a fetus develops in the womb. As time passes and the idea gets developed and fleshed out in terms of workability and application, it begins to look like the finished product.

So this is the process of remaking your life. It starts with the spark of creation: conception. Give birth first to an idea, or an attitude or a goal. Then, over time, nourish it and work with it, spend time getting to know it and feel, see and hear it. Try it on for size. See yourself as if you had already accomplished the task or goal. When you can do this, you are already more than halfway there. Continue to nurture and feed your fragile creation, until it gets strong enough to stand on its own. Then you will know that you have the power to create and manifest positive changes in your own life and the lives of others, which is the product of intercessory prayer. You will know the joy of co-creating your life and your world with God. Ask and you shall receive, speak your word, and it will be done for you by heaven. Place your confidence in God, who has never been known to be wrong or unfaithful. Claim your inheritance as a child of God and take what is already yours. Your inheritance is abundance, freedom from constant worry and heartache and the grace to live your life with joy, as God intended.

Practical Wisdom: Manifestation is thought-into-form. Thoughts create. Consistent thought, positive OR negative, is a powerful tool to effect change one person or millions. It's the courage to take risks that can bring about change in the face of resistance and also manifest the desires of one's heart into physical reality. Manifestation is a form of alchemy, which is essentially a function of quantum physics. Alchemy is

159

traditionally defined as the process of turning lead into gold. Manifestation is the process through heart-centered intention, of invoking thought energy, then through the consistent belief of faith, causing it to solidify in space and time, into form. The Bible puts it this way, in Romans 12:2: "Do not conform to the pattern of this world but be transformed by the renewing of your mind. Then you will be able to test and approve what God's will is—His good, pleasing and perfect will." (NIV).

Practical Strategy: As the essay clearly states, every project, building, social movement or work of art started with conception supported by creative intention, boosted by the heart, which is essentially the prayer of creation. You know that saying "Be careful what you pray for—you might get it?" Create carefully, deliberately and with positive intentions. The spark of an idea that begins in one's creative mind has to be fanned into flame by the heart. If the mind sets an intention but the heart isn't into it, it won't fly very far before crashing back to Earth. So if we literally have the power of creation in our lives, why not use it for our highest good and the highest good of others? Whatever change you want to make, name it, write it down, picture it in your mind or cut out pictures of it and paste them on a vision board; then fuel the flame of creation with your consistent nurturing attention. To multiply and speed up the result, join your intent with that of thousands or millions of like-minded souls. The prayer of intention said in faith (invoked) with the knowledge that according to Universal Law what we ask for is already on the way to us and that it's in the process of manifestation (thought-into-form), is a powerful prayer.

Swimming Upstream: You are Going the Wrong Way!

People think that if they have a plan for their lives, if they cover all the bases so to speak, that everything should work out for them. They get an education, marry, get a job, start a business and do any number of things in order to "secure their future." The one thing they are forgetting is that there is a spiritual plan at work in their lives as well. Call it destiny or God's will but there is a spiritual component, an underlying structure and rhythm that is perfectly timed for your growth and the growth of others in your life. Your free will allows you to access this level of being and make decisions within the context but if you go around it, you will most likely run into a wall. Let us give you an example. Suppose a woman marries, thinking that she now has security for life, through her husband. He is the provider and protector and all she has to do is keep the house and raise the children. She gives a part of herself away to him in this context because she doesn't see that she has other gifts to develop in addition to being a mother and wife. It's like putting all your eggs in one basket. If someone drops the basket or steals it, half your life is gone with it.

We understand that societal and cultural customs sometimes dictate these themes in people's lives but we would ask you to take another look. Who among you can live without food, water and air? The same thing happens to your soul when it is denied a chance to expand, to grow, to exercise its will on this Earth. You were put here for a reason and that reason is to learn universal truths. The lessons are presented against the backdrop of life. The first is love. Love one another and forgive one another as God forgives you. Do not judge, for when you judge another, you are actually judging a part of yourself. As Jesus said, "Who among you is without sin?"

Practical Wisdom: If you find yourself consistently "swimming upstream," either you're in the wrong river or you need to turn your canoe around and paddle with the current, right? So how to tell when you're caught in an emotional riptide? You find yourself saying to yourself, friends or a therapist, "Why does this keep happening to me?" That is not to say you should give up and switch partners or careers if you hit a rough patch. It also doesn't mean you should accept abuse or other harmful behavior from others. This essay is about discernment and the ability to look deeper, beneath the demands of the physical world to see God's fingerprints on the blueprint of your life. This is where "gut feeling" comes in. Are you called? If you feel that you are you probably are. If life as you know it is disintegrating around you, if nothing is working out and you find yourself in a Dark Night of the Soul, the rainbow is waiting.

Practical Strategy: In order to get to where you're going in any efficient way, you need a map. However, any map is useless unless you know your destination. If you're not sure where you want to go and how to get there, sit with the discomfort and calmly self-assess. Why are you not happy? What or who do you want in or out of your life? Is there a feeling of natural flow to your life or are you forcing yourself to march to the beat of someone else's drum? What's on your hard drive that may be keeping you from the desire of your heart? Pay particular attention to the "shoulds," "can'ts" and "what ifs." Who are the authors of those negative, limiting beliefs? Parents, teachers, religious authorities, peers with their own wounded hard drives, the relentless assault of commercials, celebrities, YouTube, Facebook and the rest of the media conglomerate? Ask for guidance from God. Sort out what YOU know, feel and want in your heart from the onslaught of advertising, Internet propaganda and fear-based "advice" competing for bandwidth in your mind. Write out a list of pros and cons, do some research, ask a trusted mentor for their input and then turn your ship in the direction you feel your current is taking you and go full speed ahead.

Terrorism, Roots of

You ask us about the roots of terrorism and we are pleased to answer you. The roots of this discontent and smoldering anger have been simmering in the pot of the Middle East for centuries. The roots were placed generations ago when one tribe rose up against the other in Jerusalem. Nothing has been the same since. Each side is more concerned with winning than justice and the fighting will continue until they realize this error. Winning for one means another must lose. This paradigm can only bring more dissension and pain into the world. You continue to be faced with escalating tensions in the world. You are desperate for peace and security yet it seems more elusive than ever before. The more you erect barriers and walls and security procedures in an effort to protect and defend, the more vulnerable you feel.

In the art of problem solving, it is necessary to go to the root cause from which all struggle, oppression and fear emanate. In this situation, the global threat of terrorism springs from multiple causes. The evil inherent in killing in the name of the Most High Holy God is first. The essence of God is love, peace, acceptance, non-judgment, forgiveness and reconciliation. The greatest commandment is to love one another as your own body. There will be from time to time throughout history, false teachers who will attempt to pervert the message of God for their own purposes. Osama bin Laden is [was] one of these. He has taken a holy text given by God to the people of the world through the Prophet Mohammed and perverted it for his own evil use.

The solutions to this present crisis can be found in the past. History is a template upon which the operating instructions for the future are inscribed. The lessons of oppression and resistance have not yet penetrated the consciousness of America nor most of the rest of the world. There are pockets of peace and tranquility in just societies around the globe but they are few and far

163

between. In the United States, the arrogance of force and power has seduced the leadership into a false sense of security. All the ships and planes and sophisticated weapons systems are no match for a more potent weapon in the hearts and minds of the people: fear. The only antidote for fear is faith, which brings inner peace and security. In this climate of oppression and injustice, there can be no peace and there will be no security until there is justice. There is no doctrine in the Holy books or in man's law that supersedes God's command to love one another.

Practical Wisdom: There has always been oppression, resistance and evil in the world. In the first recorded cover up, the Book of Genesis reports that Cain killed his brother Abel, then attempted to lie to God. Cain was caught when his brother's innocent blood cried out from the ground to God for justice. Today oppression, resistance and evil continues to spill into the world from the minds of evil men. Darkness thrives in the absence of resistance from the light.

Practical Strategy: There are no easy answers to coping with the daily onslaught of death, tragedy, murder, corruption, evil and terrorism in the world today. Some people use avoidance; the "head in the sand" approach works for them. They don't read or watch the news or they don't own a television. In that act of what they perceive to be self-protection, they're also abdicating their responsibility to stand for good, truth and justice and against aggression, evil, lies and terrorism. The only strategy that works for me and the clients I've shared it with is absolute faith and trust in God's power, protection, and provision, and when called for, advocacy. There are dozens of scriptural promises in the Bible describing our sacred covenant with God and the formidable spiritual power given to believers.

Transitions

We wish to speak tonight about transitions. The word means change, shift and hopefully growth. A transition is a step upward, a form of transformation. Transformation means a passing away of the old and a rebirth of the new. It can only mean healing and the joy that is found in peace and love.

There are many forms of transition. We transform in the physical, in terms of life and death, and we transform in our personalities, emotional states and spiritual states as well. Let us focus first on the spiritual transition or transformation.

As the heart opens, Spirit is allowed to come in, which brings light and form to the soul. The seed that is thus planted matures and ripens to burst forth like the spring leaf from the winter bud. It is a process of new growth that brings one to the next level of peace, personal power, understanding and healing.

The next form of transformation is emotional. This is when people are able to peel back the layers of their hurts and betrayals, and see the root of the emotions for what they really are. If someone has betrayed you, the weakness is within them, not you. They betrayed themselves first in order to behave that way. They created a situation of bad karma, where the cause, their betrayal, is a double-edged sword. They have to suffer the damage to their own soul for having done such an act and they have to answer to God for the pain they have caused an innocent person.

Forgiveness is the key to healing the sin of betrayal and is what actually brings the transformation about. One must transcend the emotion and look at the root cause or effect in order to get over it. Ask yourself: "What does the betrayal, this action of another person, really have to do with me? Does their betrayal and undeserving of my trust in them reflect badly on me as a person? Did I cause their betrayal?" We think that if you look closely, you will find that the answer is no.

God is always ready to forgive and to set aside your transgression. He wants us to simply admit our mistake when we get off the path, then get back on it again. We must forgive ourselves as well as others in order to transform ourselves and our circumstances. The power of forgiveness is the stuff legends are made of. Forgiveness is injected with divine power in order for it to have the healing effect on all parties that it does. Do not be afraid to make transitions in your lives. As we stated last night, break out of the glass prison and reach for the stars in your life here. Fulfill your highest and best potential. Discover your life purpose. Answer the call of Spirit and you will be aligning yourself with the most powerful force in the universe. Live a life of service to others in conjunction with your own growth and happiness and the satisfaction that only the attainment of goals can provide.

Ask God for everything. No request is too small or unimportant. Your transformation from physical being to spiritual being occurs at the moment of your physical death on this plane. Begin now to raise your vibration so that you can be prepared and ready when the time comes, as well as attaining your full potential while you still have work to do here. Live a glorious and fruitful life, for this is your inheritance as a child of the living God.

Practical Wisdom: I've had to read this essay dozens of times to let the depth of the truth and timeless wisdom sink in. One of the great mysteries of life is the nature of our consciousness/soul/spirit. Albert Einstein said, "Energy cannot be destroyed. It can only be changed from one form to another." So if energy cannot be destroyed but can only change form, then the transition from life to death is simply a change of address, isn't it? Having had a number of experiences with mediumship, I'm convinced the Spirit does survive physical death. I've had a number of stunning encounters with deceased relatives—my own and those of clients—and have had other unmistakable communications with souls who have passed over. The detailed, accurate communication and the healing and forgiveness that takes place, changes lives on both sides of the veil.

Practical Strategy: Forgiveness is one of the most difficult spiritual principals for people to understand and apply in their lives. On the surface, it seems like letting someone who hurt us get away with it and that seems unjust. Children reason this way. If something isn't fair, a parent or teacher will never hear the end of it. But as adults, we have to transcend that tug-of-war and make the decision to drop our end of the rope, turn the struggle over to God and walk away. It's not easy but it's a necessary requirement for both peace of mind and physical health. Know that the Law of Karma—and it's a law as consistently dependable as gravity whether you decide to believe in it or not—will visit those who harm others. Our job is to detach from the pain and turn the issue over to God for justice, then walk away in peace.

Part II:
Outside the Box: Practical Strategies When You're Not Sure What to Do

After reading *Anatomy of the Spirit* by medical intuitive Caroline Myss, Ph.D. and *Awakening Intuition* by Mona Lisa Schulz, MD, Ph.D., also a medical intuitive, I taught myself how to do readings by directing my attention to a client's chakra system one chakra at a time and waiting to see what impressions came to me as I scanned each one. If you want to develop your intuition, you can try this as well, with the client's permission. It is unethical and a spiritual error to scan someone's energy field without their permission, unless it's an emergency or there is some life-threatening issue at hand. Parents need to give permission for intuitive scans on a child under age 18.

My First Intuitive Reading: A Case of Dissociative Identity Disorder

The first reading I tried to do was for "Jane," a woman in her 30's who was referred to me for chronic anxiety. We talked briefly, I told her I was trying to learn how to do intuitive scans and asked if I could scan her before we got into her history. She agreed, so I went into another office, directed my intention to her chakra system beginning with the root and going up to the crown, then wrote down everything that came to me without judging, editing or reacting to it.

The initial problem was that I thought for sure I must be wrong because although I only got one line of intuitive data out of each chakra, they were all impressions and images of sexual abuse, violent rape, dissociation--, all really horrific abuse that I would classify as torture. Since I was new at this, I didn't know if the images were accurate and if they were, I wasn't sure if they were actual events or symbolic.

I went back to her and apologized because I thought I must be wrong about all this, then asked if she was ever raped. She proceed to calmly tell me that her father subjected her to incest for years, beginning when she was about three and finally ending when she left the house at 17. He threatened to kill her and her mother if she ever told anyone.

After we talked for a while, I left the room to get us both some water. When I returned, Jane was sitting quietly with her head bowed and I thought she was resting her eyes. When I spoke to her, she slowly raised her head, eyes closed and the high-pitched voice of a little girl came out of her mouth.

"My name is Amy. I'm 12. I'm really scared, can you help me?"

As I sat there momentarily stunned speechless, all I could think of was an old black and white movie starring Joanne Woodward about a woman with multiple personalities titled "The Three Faces of Eve." I began to panic because I'd never seen this before, had no idea how to get Jane back and besides it was light years beyond my fledgling scope of practice. I shut my eyes and sent up an SOS for immediate guidance. Instantly the answer came: "You have a weeping 12-year-old in front of you. Treat her."

I said to Amy, "Do you know who I am?"

She said, "Yes, you're the nice lady who helps Jane."

"That's right Amy and you and Jane are safe here with me. No one is going to hurt you, I promise. There are some angels around you right now and they're going to protect you here and when you leave and stay with you always. Can you feel their soft, warm hands?"

I had covered Jane with a blanket as she sat on the couch and her hands began to move under the blanket. "Yes, I feel their hands. They're going to protect me."

"That's right. Now I need to speak to Jane again. Can you please ask her to come back? You and I can talk again later, okay honey?"

"Okay."

Eyes still closed, Amy nodded and lowered her head while I held my breath. After a moment she raised her head, opened her eyes and there was Jane, looking confused.

Jane said, "What happened? Did I fall asleep?"

I explained to her what had just transpired and she reported being unaware of any of it. Without mentioning the textbook diagnosis that had apparently just displayed itself, I told her I needed to refer her to a clinical psychologist I knew who specialized in dissociative disorders. I gave that doctor Jane's reading and a few weeks later she invited me to come to her compound to see how Jane was doing and to observe one of her sessions.

When I arrived, Jane was cradling a baby doll, which the doctor explained was her symbolic baby self. Jane asked if I wanted to hold her baby and carefully handed it to me, supporting the head as if it was a real baby. We went into a treatment room and sat on the floor and I watched the doctor work with Jane to begin to integrate her baby self. I kept in touch with Jane and learned that she integrated several personalities and is now operating full time as Jane.

The serial abuse and terror that Jane suffered caused her psyche to split to help her survive the overwhelming violation, pain and terror of that experience. Multiple personality disorder is now called "dissociative identity disorder," DID for short. The split-off parts of the client's psyche are called "alter personalities" or "alters." If the original core personality is aware of the existence of alters and what their roles are in the inner constellation, that awareness is called being "co-conscious."

In other cases, the core personality is unaware of the existence of alters, who they are, what their roles are and what they're up to when they take over the body/mind. There are cases in the clinical literature where alters have different eye colors than the host personality, which means when the alter surfaces, the eye color changes and when the alter goes back inside, the eye color changes back to what it was. Alters have been found to have different handwriting, to be left-handed when the core personality is right-handed, to speak languages the host person doesn't know and to exhibit other fascinating attributes that there's no explanation for in the client's history or experience. Some alters can be dangerous. Some of them are protectors but other ones can carry the rage of the core person's pain and victimization and can harm the body or harm other people when in a dissociated state. A person with alters needs to be treated by a psychiatrist or clinical psychologist with specialized training in complex trauma and dissociation. Dissociative Identity Disorder is exceedingly rare and some psychiatrists don't believe in it but the two cases I've seen in my private practice were unmistakably genuine.

There's another body of work that explains DID as one form of spiritual possession, in which a disembodied human soul or a supernatural entity or demon takes over or interferes with a person's mind. One fascinating 600-page book, *Remarkable Healings*, by psychiatrist Shakuntala Modi, M.D., discusses various spiritual causes for physical and emotional illness, including some cases of schizophrenia. According to the author, past-lives and various sources of entity or demonic attachment or possession can cause what appear to be mental or physical illness but which is really supernatural interference. There are gifted, very experienced psychic healers who are able to remove demonic and other supernatural entity interference and I refer cases to them when I discern it. That is a specialty that takes training, skill and spiritual power to perform. Having been unpleasantly attacked a few times by entities attached to some clients, which I needed help to release in spite of having, I thought, engaged proper psychic protection, I would caution readers to not attempt to perform any "extractions," exorcisms or deliverance (in the evangelical Christian tradition). The Catholic Church also deals with exorcism, but it can be done without the formalities that entails.

A Mind Shattered by Ritual Abuse and Overwhelming Terror

This is a phone reading for another person who also had DID. "Samantha," another victim of serial incest, rape and ritual abuse had been diagnosed by a psychiatrist but that doctor was unable to integrate her. The phone reading done while knowing only her name and age shows how the damage from this overwhelming trauma has ricocheted through her body and mind. After the reading, Samantha told me she knew she had DID and was aware of the alter personalities inside her, what their names were and what they were doing for her and in some cases to her. She was also referred to Jane's doctor.

Overview: Severe dysfunction in family of origin. Brutal abuse by father. Mother did not protect. Client was the "target" child or "container child" in the family.

1) "I wasn't wanted" Container for your father's rage. Took the abuse to "protect" siblings? Feeling of martyrdom. "I'm the strong one, I can take it, I have to protect the others." Raped, images of sexual abuse, a small girl lying face down on a bed. Image of a pet, maybe a puppy being killed in front of you-- did this happen or is this symbolic? "I won't survive this." "I want to die, life isn't worth living." "I can't protect myself." "What did I do to deserve this?"

2) A vacant, black hole in 2nd chakra. Gutted and disempowered. "I have to hang on, just to survive." Fear, anxiety, dread, waiting for the other shoe to drop feeling. Tiptoeing around to try to avoid abuse. Was father an alcoholic? "I'll never be the same again. Everything has been taken from me. I'm empty, I'm all used up." Out of body, dissociation during abuse, image of you floating above and

looking down at yourself and the scene. Images of more than one person abusing you; was this a case of ritual abuse?

3) Parts are split. Image of you standing in the center of a circle and other children looking at you but they're parts of you. One feels like a boy alter. "I had to escape the pain." "Part of me is gone." Wandering. Lost feeling. Fear, dread it could happen again.

4) Imagery of a Valentine heart with a primary wound, a black spot in the center and the heart is broken into pieces and the pieces are separated. It looks like an explosion went off in the center of the heart and the heart is shattered. The pieces are frozen in place.

5) Image of a rope or cord around the neck, again, is this real or symbolic? Don't speak, don't tell, don't scream, be silent. It's not safe to speak. Feeling of being strangled, gasping for breath.

6) Imagery of the mind as a room and you're in the farthest part of the room away from the doorway, deep in the center of the room. Symbolic of the wounding that is being held in your center. The child is hiding in there, doesn't want to be seen; it feels safe to hide deep in the center. She's wary and needs to protect herself.

7) Conflict with God. Is part of you blaming God for the abuse, for not saving you? Do you feel abandoned by God? Confusion. Why did God allow this to happen to me?

Some books dealing with dissociative identity disorder are in the bibliography, including *First Person Plural*, a fascinating account of DID from the viewpoint of a man who as a child was subjected to incest by his mother, which caused his psyche to fracture into many alters. He later recovered and became a psychologist.

Chronic Stress from Dysfunctional Relationships Can Make Us Sick

The following reading was done in 2012 for a woman who at age 62 had cancer. She presented as strangely childlike and naïve. After handing her a copy of the reading, she revealed that she had been in an emotionally destructive on again, off again relationship for several years with a man who sounded to me like a sociopath or at least a malignant narcissist. He expected her to meet all his needs without question and be at his beck and call day and night no matter what she was doing or how she was feeling, even though she was undergoing rounds of chemotherapy and was fighting for her life. He continually berated her, told her she was selfish (for having needs of her own) and threatened abandonment whenever she tried to speak up for herself, all the while telling her he loved her. I pleaded with her repeatedly to leave him because his emotional abuse was such a drain on her power and energy I knew she could never get well as long as he was in her life. She refused. Although we did some deep work, she died in 2014. Here is her reading.

Overview: Rejection and sabotage by others has characterized much of your life. You have a pattern of attracting users and perpetrators who are only too happy to take advantage of your good nature. There's a certain naïveté in you that allows this. There's a childlike trust about you that opens you to being taken advantage of in various ways. Do you find that you tend to trust people too quickly and it doesn't work out well? "I just want to be happy and I want everyone to be happy." Sounds like a wistful Pollyanna part of you; do you recognize her energy inside you? You are a humanitarian at heart, always trying to see the good in others but not getting what you want and need in return.

1) Root chakra "I was violated." Shock and disbelief on the face of a child. This is the first time your trust was shattered. "I never saw it coming, nobody protected me. I was all alone." Dissociation; it appears that you were shocked out of your body, looks to be about age 5. Betrayal and abandonment. A sense of disconnect from self within yourself. Do you sense this? Imagery of you standing on a trap door and it suddenly opens beneath you and you fall through.

2) Navel: "I've lost my way." Did you attach yourself to men and other relationships as a way of trying to find your identity? It appears that you're still looking, as in, "Who am I?" There's a part of you that's afraid to step out into the world and be seen. You haven't yet found your niche, so to speak, or your mission. The lack of self-confidence and identity is holding back the expression of this power.

3) Solar Plexus: Indecisiveness, anxiety, lack of self-confidence, imagery of you tiptoeing around others so as to not rock the boat. Do you resonate with being a people pleaser? If so, this is a defense against more rejection and abandonment. "I have to be who others want me to be." Self-image and self-worth, confidence are not fully engaged.

4) Heart: A pattern of self-sacrifice, giving yourself away. You don't want others to be deprived and to hurt the way you did. Again, you hope that by giving of yourself, others will give back to you but it doesn't often happen that way.

5) Throat: You choose your words carefully so as to not invoke any controversy. You go along to get along in meetings. There's a survival level fear in this chakra, again, rooted in fear of abandonment, which to a child carries the energy of death. You hesitate to speak your truth because what if others don't agree?

6) Mind: You're interested in higher forms of wisdom, are a spiritual seeker but a sense of inadequacy and unworthiness

176

holds you back from true communion with the divine. Imagery of you sticking your toe into a pool, testing the waters. The mask you wear with others hides your fear and shame. Who shamed you? Confusion.

7) Connection to the Divine: Were you raised in a traditional, structured religion? It appears that you're viewing God from a safe distance, unwilling or not knowing how to connect. There's a quality of being on the outside looking in, feeling that you'd be unwelcome. Again, this seems to connect to the circuit of abandonment and rejection that appears to have started in childhood. On a subconscious level, God is very parent-like and that's scary or intimidating for a person who had an emotional disconnect with parent(s). "I just want to serve!" Frustration.

Eight Years of Panic Attacks Rooted in a Traumatic Birth

An Army officer in his 40s I'll call "Roy" came to see me because he had suffered from chronic, unprovoked "uncued" panic attacks for over eight years. He had been to a psychiatrist, a psychologist, therapists and even ministers seeking relief that continued to elude him. An uncued panic attack is one that comes on suddenly, without warning and without any discernable trigger. One can wake up in a panic or stroll out to the roadside mailbox and get hit with one or suddenly have a panic attack while driving. The uncued version is especially terrifying because in the absence of any obvious triggers, the victim and others around him have no idea when an attack will strike since there's no specific trigger to avoid to try to prevent them.

If a person has claustrophobia for example, he or she can avoid elevators and manage the trigger through avoidance but victims of uncued attacks feel helpless and vulnerable all the time. The constant anxiety ignites the release of the hormones cortisol, adrenalin and norepinephrine as stress ricochets through the sympathetic nervous system. The adrenal glands (small endocrine glands that sit atop each kidney) can get stuck on "fight or flight" from pumping out the stress hormones that unbalance the nervous system. Unless the stress is managed, gut issues may begin such as irritable bowel that can deepen into ulcerative colitis. Chronic pain such as migraine headaches and fibromyalgia may result, chronic fatigue may arise, immunity can be compromised and it all sets off a daisy chain of emotional and physical dysfunction that can lead to serious illness in the long term.

Roy had, like hundreds of thousands of other American panic attack sufferers, made dozens of trips to the emergency room thinking he was having a heart attack, only to be checked out for cardiac problems, diagnosed with panic disorder and released with another prescription for anti-anxiety medication which he didn't want but had to take in order to function.

Panic disorder is very debilitating and scary. I've only had a couple and they were horrible. Clients tell me it feels like they're going to die. For eight years Roy had to carefully map out his route when traveling anywhere to make sure he knew where the nearest fire station or hospital emergency room was. Traveling anywhere, especially on a plane, required heavy sedation.

I didn't do a full intuitive scan on Roy but as I "tuned in" to him, I asked about the thoughts and feelings that come over him when the panic strikes. He said, "I'm suffocating; I'm dying and the whole world is dying." I asked about repetitive dreams. He had a series of dreams that started as a child and continued into his teen years that had a common theme: being trapped in a small space— a toy box with the lid shut that he couldn't open or a suitcase that was locked. Always the feeling was the same: trapped, suffocating, stuck, feeling like he was dying, out of control, a perception of darkness and feeling terrified. As I listened "between the lines," the metaphorical dream imagery of the small spaces seemed to me to be metaphors for a birth canal and traumatic birth or a past life "bleed through." The energetic signatures of a rough delivery were very strong.

I said to Roy, "This has birth trauma written all over it. Call your mother."

On speakerphone, Mom reported that she was in labor for three days with him. He was stuck, so rather than do a C-section, they finally yanked him out with forceps.

Can you imagine what being stuck and struggling for survival for three days, then being dragged out of his mother's body with metal forceps must have been like? It would feel like a panic attack—terrifying and life-threatening. His tender nervous system and brain were already under a chemical assault from whatever drugs and anesthesia they gave his mother in addition to the stress hormones flooding her body from her own fear and pain. All that on top of the physical trauma of the violent forceps delivery on a helpless baby encoded chemically induced shock, emotional overwhelm and fear of survival in his fragile brain and nervous system.

Roy used Tapas Acupressure Technique (TAT) one of the energy psychology self-healing methods listed in the Resources section, to heal himself as I guided him. The TAT was combined with guided imagery narrated by me to contact, dialogue with and rescue/recover his still terrified dissociated baby self from the delivery process, then gently re-deliver him back into present time and a safe reunion/integration with adult Roy.

In a testament to the accuracy of the term mind/body connection, at the end of our session Roy placed his hand on his solar plexus and commented that he might need some physical therapy to learn how to function with relaxed abs. He made a fist and held it over the center of his stomach, then slowly opened his fingers.

"My stomach muscles have never been relaxed. I've just lived with this tension and pressure all my life. Now that it's gone, I'll have to get used to the feeling."

I explained that Roy was experiencing the physical release of fear energy that had been stuck inside his body and encoded in his brain for over 40 years.

I've kept in touch with Roy and at this writing it's been eight years since our single 90-minute session. He's never had another panic attack, cued or uncued.

"Energy cannot be created or destroyed; it can only be changed from one form to another."

~ Albert Einstein

Energy and the Soul: What Does the Research Say?

From a psychological standpoint, *dissociation* can be defined as detachment, disconnection and/or separation of one's conscious awareness from the body and from present time due to traumatic physical or emotional helplessness and overwhelm. From a spiritual or consciousness standpoint, I define it additionally as when a part of our non-physical self, our consciousness, spirit or soul, *is one dimension away.* Dissociation is one example of being one dimension away; death is apparently another, and out of body experiences such as shamanic journeying and soul retrieval clearly take us into another dimension of consciousness.

Try as they might, pioneering researchers from neuroscience to quantum physics have as yet been unable to definitively define consciousness or pin down a definition of the mind. I can't either but I suspect that during a dissociative episode, our consciousness is the soul/spirit part of us that, in a protective effort to ensure our emotional and in some cases physical survival, opens an escape hatch that moves our conscious awareness *one dimension away* from the terror and overwhelm of a present time traumatic experience.

Is human consciousness part of the human soul or perhaps another name for the soul? Nobody knows for sure. My opinion is that the aspect of us that is non-physical consciousness/soul/spirit and which is capable of dissociation is the same aspect that leaves our body at death. *Clearly, the mind is not the same as the brain.* The brain is physical cell tissue; the mind is the seat of consciousness that resides not only in the brain but is also non-local. Non-local refers to psychic realms such as clairvoyance, remote viewing and distance healing. Energy follows thought. Thought precedes energy. The process of manifestation is thought-energy into form, either physical form or an outcome, such as healing, via focused intention, which is another definition of prayer. The mind animates the brain as shown on an MRI scan. When the brain reacts to a drug or traumatic memory, different parts of the brain "light up" on the MRI. At the same time, there may also be an emotional and/or physical response. This is why when we bring to mind a traumatic memory, we can usually feel pressure, pain or a subtle awareness in one or more parts of the body correlated to that memory. If we reverse the process and notice pain, tension or dysfunction in the body, that is a somatic memory—the energetic imprint of a traumatic memory that is encoded in the body and which releases when the emotional charge is released in the limbic brain.

A stroke destroys particular parts of cellular brain function just as a heart attack destroys heart muscle. Coma can be described as a state of suspended animation. The physical body is alive, the brain is alive, but the person is unconscious. Their awareness is "off line" and they may be in an extended out-of-body state. There are reports of some psychics and shamans who are able to "find" the consciousness of a person in a coma, bring them back to present time and the body, and they wake up, Sometimes even after months or years, the brain heals enough for the coma to lift. The person wakes up and is once again in present time. When the late actor Christopher Reeve broke his neck in a horseback riding accident and was permanently paralyzed from the neck down, he remained conscious, able to reason and feel emotions. He asked his wife if he should be allowed to die and she said, "No. You're still you." The consciousness/soul/spirit is an expression of the God force, the spark of life, the animation, in all living things. No one can measure the timeline of the soul but I believe it's limitless and eternal. The fascinating phenomena of spontaneous body memories as well as fears, phobias and repetitive dreams that are traced to past-lives speak to the timeline of the soul in what appears to be reincarnation.

Terrified of Abandonment from the Womb

One day a woman I'd been working with called for help with her 18-month-old granddaughter. Whenever anyone outside the family came to the house, the baby would scream in terror. No one knew why, so the grandmother and her daughter, the baby's mother, brought her to my office. I scanned the baby and picked up strong anxiety due to fear of abandonment. The mother confessed that she was distraught because her marriage was not going well and for several months during the pregnancy she thought about giving the baby up for adoption. It wasn't until the eighth month that she decided to keep her. I explained that because of the mother's dominant, repetitive fear thoughts about adoption, the baby had been imprinted energetically with the fear of abandonment, which to a child equals fear of death. We sat down and put the baby on the floor between us where she happily played with some toys. Then the grandmother, the mother and I did surrogate EFT tapping on ourselves as if we were the baby and had experienced her abandonment and survival level fear. About two weeks later, the grandmother reported that the baby was non-reactive to strangers and had even allowed the waitress at Sunday brunch to pick her up. There were no further episodes of stranger-danger panic.

Quantum Healing: Past Lives and Phantom Limb Pain

As a Christian, I initially rejected reincarnation out of hand but after doing some research on the ancient shamanic practice of "soul retrieval" and some aspects of the Native American tradition, my skepticism began to soften. In the book *Voices from the Womb*, a psychologist used regression hypnosis to take adults back to their time in the womb and asked them specific questions about it. The psychologist was able to verify much of the information his patients reported under hypnosis by interviewing their parents about life during the pregnancy, as well as reviewing medical records. In subsequent sessions with clients like Roy, it became clear to me that consciousness exists in pre-verbal states. If that was so, then trauma could also be treated by accessing the dissociated consciousness of a person's pre-verbal state though hypnosis or guided imagery. My energy psychology colleague, psychologist Wendy Ann McCarty, Ph.D.,R.N, specializes in research and work with pre-verbal trauma. To learn more, you'll find a link to her web site, Wondrous Beginnings, in the Resources section.

My skepticism about past lives began to shift after reading accounts of small children who remember detailed, verifiable accounts of past lives. There are a few books on the subject listed on Amazon. One case really got my attention. The story of a little boy named James Leininger from a conservative Christian family in southern Louisiana was profiled on the ABC News magazine Primetime in April 2004. His parents wrote a book about their experiences with him and how they gradually, after a lot of research and skepticism, came to accept that he's the reincarnated spirit of a WWII pilot named James Huston Jr. At age two, little James began to awaken with terrifying nightmares of being trapped in and crashing a burning plane that he was piloting over

Iwo Jima, it was later determined. It's an amazing story, including the time when young James and his father attended a reunion of the remaining pilots from James Huston's WWII squadron. One of the veterans came up to James and his father and the man asked the boy, "Do you know who I am?" James replied with the man's name and said he knew it because he recognized the man's voice. Needless to say, they had never met. There's more on this case on YouTube and Amazon.

Any remaining skepticism on my part evaporated after treating dozens of people who had been everywhere and tried everything to get over some kind of panic, phobia or emotional pattern plaguing them, only to find closure after healing past life trauma. Does that prove that past lives exist? No, but it establishes a very interesting cause and effect connection.

The Bible says we only live once, so I asked a highly respected internationally known Christian Bishop for his opinion. I described a couple of sessions in which clients appeared to be re-experiencing past life trauma, then reported some clairvoyant glimpses and physical sensations that appeared to originate in a past life of my own. He remarked with a smile, "The Bible has been through a lot of editing in 2000 years." I then pointed out that according to many eye-witness accounts recorded in the Bible, Christ himself came back from the dead. He agreed.

Hoarding: The Metaphors Behind the Madness

"Eric," a successful businessman in his early 50s, came to my office burdened with a shameful secret. He reluctantly admitted that no one had been inside his home for over a decade. Unlike many hoarders, Eric was not in denial. He nervously handed me a stack of photographs of his home and garage in an upscale neighborhood. Piles of books and stacks of files and papers littered every surface and the two-car garage was stacked nearly to the ceiling with more cardboard boxes of files.

I "read" the *energetic signature* of Eric's situation by interpreting the symbolism or metaphor being expressed through his hoarding.

"Okay, so you're saving information. You can get information on the Internet and scan important documents and store them on a hard drive. Why are you saving all this information?"

Eric looked bewildered. "Information? I never looked at it that way before. I don't know why, I just know I HAVE to."

As we looked at each other, I began to see images of what looked like a stockade made of logs. I mentioned to Eric what was coming to me and he said he'd had repetitive dreams about a stockade. Being that dreams are sometimes expressions of the unconscious, I figured we were onto something. As the picture expanded, I began to see various scenes of what looked like 1800s America and also perceived the back story about the stockade.

"I see you in a settlement with other people, men and women, and they're dressed in what looks like colonial American clothes. They're worried about attacks from the local Native Americans.

You're the leader of this group. At some point, the settlement was attacked and you died and the others died because you *didn't have the information* that the attack was coming. You were responsible for protecting those people and you failed. So apparently your hoarding of information is a bleed through of trauma from that lifetime into this one. Part of your subconscious is determined to never be caught off-guard again."

As Eric thought this over, he was suddenly overcome with emotion. He also recognized a pattern of taking the blame and allowing others to make him feel guilty about events in relationships that upon further examination were not his fault. He said, "Maybe this is why I've felt so guilty my whole life. It feels like I owe some kind of debt just for being alive.

We did some energy work to neutralize the past life trauma, then worked on the aspects that were showing up in his life and relationships. Within a month, he had cleaned out his house and no longer felt the need to gather and store information or sacrifice himself in relationships.

30 Years of Phantom Pain Gone in One Session

There are lots of things in this world and in the fields of medicine, psychology, energy medicine and quantum physics that can't be explained or even measured accurately at this time, for example phantom limb pain. Phantom limb pain is the sometimes severe, intractable pain that follows amputation of a limb or body part. There's no effective treatment for it in the medical model. Doctors have tried surgical interventions and other procedures aimed at the part of the brain or spinal nerves that govern the missing limb or part and that doesn't help the pain. In some cases only heavy-duty narcotic painkillers blunt the agony and also blunt the patient's life.

The reason that medical interventions don't work for phantom limb pain is that it's an energy field. Seen clairvoyantly, the stump is hemorrhaging energy like a faucet left wide open. The way to stop the hemorrhaging and the pain is A) treat the trauma that resulted in the amputation with an energy-based method to neutralize the encoded trauma from the injury that's still stuck in the body/mind and B) place an energetic "cap" on the stump to seal off the gushing energy that's trying to find and fill the etheric limb that's no longer there in physical form.

In 2003 I treated a man in his late 60s who had lost his right leg just below the knee in a car accident 30 years prior. His phantom pain was excruciating and he found little or no relief in medications. One session of EFT tapping released the trauma of the car accident and his resulting anger at the driver who hit him and the doctors who nearly killed him in a series of medical mishaps that followed. We also worked on some grief and sadness over how his life had changed, how he still missed his leg and some residual anger, regret and self-blame about not being more careful when he walked into the street from between two parked cars and was hit. Some hands-on healing to cap the energy flow gushing from his stump completed the 90-minute session and he left pain-free.

He reported an incident about a year later where he slipped on cement in the rain and banged his stump, which caused the phantom pain to return. He did a couple of rounds of EFT tapping about that, the pain stopped and he is still pain-free at this writing. If any pain starts to come back up, he does more EFT tapping to re-balance his energy system and the pain recedes. As an unfortunate postscript, my client's nephew happened to be a doctor working at the VA in San Diego. I finally called him to politely ask if he was curious about the sudden disappearance of his uncle's phantom pain, being that amputations are a signature injury in combat troops. He said, "I was happy to see that he had no further pain but we're working on drug trials here."

What I've learned from treating hundreds of people who had some form of dissociation, is that when trauma escalates to a level that the victim can't handle it physically, emotionally or spiritually and their consciousness disconnects from present time, they need to be brought back into present time in order to heal completely. That's one reason why cognitive therapy and "counseling" for trauma victims doesn't have a high success rate because the traumatized part of the victim's consciousness has fled into a time/space continuum that conventional talking therapy can't reach. Sometimes a skilled hypnotherapist, regression therapy practitioner or shaman who uses guided imagery can reach that place. Sometimes the wounding is on the soul level and requires soul retrieval of parts of our spirit.

Trauma is imprinted into the brain, mind, body and spirit and it stays there until it's accessed, brought into conscious awareness and released. Just because a fetus, a newborn, a stroke victim or someone in a coma for example, has no language or can't speak and appears to be "not there," doesn't mean they're immune to trauma.

Birth Without Violence author Dr. Frederick Leboyer realized that birth can be traumatizing for newborns, so he created a method that minimizes the normally harsh hospital delivery room environment. Low lighting, whispers and being born in water then immediately held close by the mother had babies smiling after birth instead of screaming in terror. Having a non-violent start to life is a good thing.

Murdered for Stealing the Food from the Children: A Past Life Knife in My Back

One day a professional colleague came to see me for help with food sensitivities of unexplained origin. She was allergic to basic foods that are in a lot of prepared foods: salt, butter, and wheat. I did an intuitive scan on her and other than some childhood trauma, there were no direct connections we could find. As we were discussing things, a flash of clairvoyance prompted me to casually remark, "I see you in a castle." Immediately she broke out in hysterical sobs and at that moment, what felt like an etheric dagger stabbed me in the right mid-back, just above my right kidney. The sudden intensely sharp pain made me gasp and I leaned forward and to the left, my right hand grasping my back. The pain was a high 8 out of 10. As she sobbed, "I was murdered for stealing food from the children!" a slow-motion slide show began to cross a screen in my mind.

The scene looked like medieval Europe. I saw her in that lifetime as an older male dressed in raggedy clothes. There was some kind of famine so food was scarce. There was a big pile of grain stored in a structure that looked like a barn and it was there to be rationed to the people. She (he) was caught stealing some grain and was stabbed in the back and killed. For the next 30 minutes while I squirmed in my chair holding my back, we processed that past life memory with a chakra-based healing method. She said things that she was seeing or feeling from that inner time capsule and I did as well. Finally we were able to move the energy of that event out of her energy field and when we concluded, she felt peaceful and my back pain disappeared. Two weeks later she came back for another session and reported that all her food sensitivities had disappeared

.

Appendix

Practical Strategy: Choosing a therapist or energy practitioner, licensed or not

Energy healing, spiritual healing, medical intuition, coaching and a huge menu of alternative and holistic modalities do not require a license in most states and do not require specific training or licensing to practice or teach. However, as I pointed out earlier, a degree and a professional license is no guarantee of competence, ethics or safety either. So the best thing to do when searching for a holistic practitioner is to ask for referrals from people you know and trust and then check references to find out as much as you can about education, training, certification if any and scope of practice, before seeing someone. Ask for a free consultation, which many practitioners offer. Trust your gut and tune in to your intuition as well. If something feels uncomfortable to you, trust that and go elsewhere.

Practical Strategy: Clearing Psychological Reversals, also known as "stoppers"

See the list of resources below to find an energy psychology practitioner to coach you if you need some help learning to self-apply EFT or if your issues involve childhood abuse, torture, dissociation, sexual abuse/rape, combat trauma or other intense emotional memories. Another reason it's a good idea to work with an experienced practitioner when handling issues that are highly emotionally charged is because it's hard to be in your head figuring out how to tap your way through a traumatic memory and feel your emotions at the same time. Having said that, the acupressure tapping methods, Emotional Freedom Technique (EFT), Thought-Field Therapy (TFT), Tapas Acupressure

Technique (TAT) and some of the other energy psychology methods are designed to be self-administered but I highly recommend not trying to take yourself through the worst things that have ever happened to you. Enlist the help of a competent practitioner and let them coach you as you process it safely to minimize re-traumatization.

EFT is not supposed to hurt. It's natural for people to cry when releasing sad memories but as the emotional charge is released from the limbic brain and neutralized through EFT tapping for example, the sadness doesn't come up again when the same memory is accessed after treatment.

With the exception of some colleagues, licensed and unlicensed, who I know to be well-trained, ethical and competent, I can't vouch for the qualifications or competency of practitioners on these lists. Ask for references, number of years of experience and scope of practice, training and/or certification and then trust your gut. There are people, both licensed and unlicensed, who in my experience are dangerously incompetent, lack proper ethical and professional boundaries, have not done their own inner work and should not be in practice at all. Some of their clients have come to me and I've seen the damage these therapists and practitioners have done.

There's an unauthorized mutation of Emotional Freedom Technique that goes by the name "Faster EFT" that's re-traumatizing on purpose, which real EFT is not. A number of people have reported unethical practices and emotionally damaging sessions, so I recommend that you avoid "FasterEFT."

Every client is vulnerable—emotionally because of their issues as well as by the inherent power differential between therapist or practitioner and client. When I was in school, one of the teachers used to bring in the quarterly report of disciplinary actions the California State Board of Behavioral Sciences issued against licensed psychologists, social workers and marriage/family therapists. He pointed out that the majority of the male therapists were being disciplined or losing their licenses for sexual violations and most of the women were in trouble for issues involving money.

Certification in an energy psychology method is a good sign in that it requires a basic level of knowledge and expertise but certification is not a guarantee of competence. Many licensed mental health clinicians have integrated energy psychology into their therapeutic toolbox. Some use it openly, others behind closed doors. State laws vary as to scope of practice. In California we have SB (Senate Bill) 577, which is an open consent law that allows consumers access to alternative practitioners as long as certain parameters are met, which are on a consent form that consumers must sign and practitioners retain. Some EFT and energy healing practitioners only see clients locally and others work by phone or Skype anywhere in the world.

To clear reversals (blocks to healing or changing,), tap the side of the hand (karate chop point) while repeating the reversals you want to clear; and when you've finished naming and tapping, add, "I deeply and completely love and accept myself, I choose to honor and respect myself and I forgive myself for any part I may have played in (the problem) and I forgive (names of people) for (whatever part they played or specify whatever they did.) In most people, clearing reversals at the beginning of any work will lower the level of emotional charge attached to a particular memory on the 0-10 intensity scale by 2-3 points.

There are many ways to learn EFT, TAT, Havening or some of the other energy psychology "power therapies." YouTube videos are a good way to start. No matter what the subject is on an EFT video you're watching, you can bookmark in your own mind an issue you want to release, whether it's a physical dysfunction or some kind of pain; then tap along with whatever the subject of the video is clearing and you should get results on your own bookmarked issues. This EFT technique is called "borrowing benefits."

For example, there's a rather graphic video clip on my web site that shows a Navy Corpsman who served in Iraq using EFT tapping with me to release a traumatic childhood memory that triggered him into previously diagnosed PTSD in Iraq. He had witnessed a murder/suicide at age 10 that came rushing back at age 20 in Iraq when he was called to bring a body bag to the scene of a service member suicide that he didn't witness. That event in the line of duty lit up the "circuit" of unresolved trauma in his brain and body that was stored for 10 years. The video shows us releasing the traumatic emotional charge from that memory in one session.

So if you have an issue, from a traumatic memory of your own to a craving for potato chips, write it down and give it a movie title, for example "The time the teacher embarrassed me in class." Then rate the emotional charge on that memory you still feel when you think about it now, from 0 which means it is neutral and has no emotional sting at all, to a 10, which is very highly charged. Write down the emotions you still feel, i.e. anger, sadness, shame, etc. and where you feel the resistance or pressure in your body, if you know. Then start tapping with your attention and words aimed at those issues and you should feel measurably better fast.

Here is a list of psychological reversals, also known as "stoppers," that can block healing or change. Reversals can be conscious or subconscious. Our energy can literally reverse and flow backwards or scramble when we try to move forward with one or more reversals still on our hard drive. Most people, if they tune in, can perceive some inner resistance that comes up when they try to heal, change or move their lives in a new direction. Reversals, again, blocks to healing or changing, have to be cleared using EFT—acupressure tapping on emotional release points on the face, hands and trunk—or another energy-based method.

It's essential to clear or neutralize them because no matter how strong your intention to do or not do something, your energy system will defeat you if you have reversals embedded in your conscious or subconscious mind. The high failure rate with maintaining a diet or exercise program using willpower is a good example of this. To clear reversals, tap the fleshy outside edge of the palm of your hand, the part you would use in a karate chop, while saying: "Even though (say the reversal) I accept myself I'm doing the best I can" or another self-affirming statement. Some people say, "I choose to honor and accept myself. I'm a good person and I'm doing the best I can" or "I choose to love and accept myself, even though I have this problem. It's just where I am right now."

For example, "Even though part of me believes it's not safe to get over this fear of flying, I accept myself. I'm doing the best I can." Or, "Even though I'm craving sugar right now, I accept myself even though I have this craving."

A good way to clear the reversals is to just tap through the list rather than trying to diagnose which ones you might have. Tapping through reversals you don't have doesn't harm anything; you can just plow through them, clearing any you might have that might be subconscious as well as those you're aware of feeling as pressure or tension in the body, resistance, anxiety, avoidance etc.

"Even though (state reversal and the issue) I accept myself, I'm a good person and this is just where I am right now." Example: "Even though *I don't want to get over my fear of flying*, I accept myself, I'm a good person and this is just where I am right now."

1) I don't want to get over...... (state the problem or issue)

2) It's not safe if I get over ....

3) I don't deserve to get over ....

4) I won't give myself permission (allow myself) to get over............

5) It won't benefit me to get over....................

6) It won't benefit others for me to get over................

7) It's impossible for me to get over....................

8) I won't get over..................................

9) I won't do what I have to do to get over........................ (this is the sabotage reversal)

10) I'm too afraid of what might happen if I get over this...................

11) I'm too angry to get over this............................

12) I don't know how to ever get over this............................

13) Bad things will happen if I get over this............................

14) I'll have to forgive people if I get over this............................

15) It wasn't fair and there's no justice but I choose to get over it anyway...............

16) Others will be disappointed if I get over this............................

17) Things might get worse if I get over............................

18) I'm not smart enough to get over............................

The following reversals are common to addictions, including weight problems, compulsions, OCD and many traumatic patterns and PTSD:

1) I'll be deprived if I get over............................

2) I'll lose my identity if I get over ....

3) I'll be confused if I get over........................

4) I'll be ashamed, humiliated, embarrassed if I get over ....

5) I'll be (blamed, criticized, judged) if I get over............................

6) I'll hate myself if I get over............................

7) I'll hurt myself if I get over............................

8) I'll misuse it if I get over............................

9) Even though I'll have to step up to the plate and take responsibility for my life and my choices.............. I deeply and completely accept myself. I'm a good person and I'm doing the best I can.

10) I'm afraid of how my life will change if I heal (release) this problem (forgive this person etc.).

For sexual abuse and PTSD (Post-traumatic Stress Disorder), here are some common specific reversals:

1) I'll be too vulnerable if I get over this.....................

2) I could get victimized again if I get over this.............

3) I'll be a target if I let this go................................

4) I'll be betrayed (used, violated) again if I get over this...............

5) I'd be a fool to let this go............................

6) They'll win if I get over this.........................

7) I'll have to forgive people if I get over this............

8) I'll be abandoned if I get over this................

9) I'm not supposed to get over this.....................

10) It's not right for me to get over this.....................

11) I'll feel too guilty if I get over this.........................

12) I'm afraid of making a mistake if I get over this..............

13) I'll be considered selfish if I get over this.....................

14) I'll be leaving others behind if I get over this................

15) I'll be rejected if I get over this...............................

16) I'll be lonely and alone if I get over this........................

17) I can't let this go..

18) I'm too damaged to ever heal this...........................

19) I might become powerful and successful if I heal this...................

20) I'll be empty if I heal this........................

21) Nothing will do any good...............................

22) I've been this way for too long and I'll never be any different................

23) Something's in the way of my clearing this problem...........................

24) I'll be punished if I get over this............................

25) Bad things will happen if I get over this...........................

26) God will punish me if I get over this...................

27) I'm an object.......................

A Final Note

We're all, whether we're aware of it or not, on a journey of learning and soul ascension. The soul's subtle promptings to treat others with kindness, tolerance, love, forgiveness and non-judgment is not dependent on religion, income, race, gender, culture or any other criteria. I hope that the spiritual guidance, practical wisdom and practical strategies presented here will enrich your life and encourage you to chart your own course, regardless of what sort of emotional scar tissue you carry. No matter what has happened to you in the past and no matter what your fears are in the present or the future, remember this: *you probably won't die from it*. If you launch a new project or relationship you might have to contend with abandonment, betrayal, humiliation, injustice, rejection and/or fear but what's the worst that can happen? You might fail and learn to do it better the next time? People might criticize you? What if you assess the risk and follow your intuition anyway? It could lead to disappointment, then again it could lead to spectacular success and happiness. When you feel paralyzed with fear and are drowning in a sea of self-doubt, say to yourself, "This feels outside my comfort zone but I won't die from it and I'm going to step out in faith and do it anyway." Pray for guidance, wait for the answer and move forward knowing that heaven has your back.

Will You Pay It Forward?

If you enjoyed *Spiritual Compass*, I'd be grateful if you would click over to Amazon and gift me <u>with a review</u>. I'd be honored to receive your unique perspective on how this book, the first of a series, touched your life and supported your spiritual path.

If someone you know is feeling lost and alone or if they're struggling with trauma, a broken heart or illness, please send them to Amazon or gift them a copy.

If you'd like to receive free bonus materials from this book and get an invitation only preview of the next two books in the Spiritual Compass series, plus receive discounted invitations to future webinars, retreats and events, sign up for my newsletter at www.suehannibal.com. You can also follow me on Twitter@SueHannibal.

Love one another. Kindness is free.

Bibliography

Allison, R. (1999) *Minds in Many Pieces: Revealing the Spiritual Side of Multiple Personality Disorder*, Paso Robles, CA, CIE Publishing

Clark, T. (1993) *More Than One: An Inside Look at Multiple Personality Disorder*, Nashville, TN, Oliver-Nelson Books

Gabriel, M. (1992) *Voices from the Womb: Consciousness and Trauma in the Pre-Birth Self*, Fairfield, CT, Aslan Publishing

Herman, J. (1997) *Trauma and Recovery: The Aftermath of Violence from Domestic Abuse to Political Terror*, New York, NY, Basic Books

Klimo, J. (1998) *Channeling: Investigations on Receiving Information from Paranormal Sources*, Berkeley, CA, North Atlantic Books

Modi, S. (1997) *Remarkable Healings: A Psychiatrist Discovers Unsuspected Roots of Mental and Physical Illnesses*, Charlottesville, VA, Hampton Roads

West, C. (2013) *First Person Plural: My Life as a Multiple*, New York, NY, Hyperion

Resources for Healing and Energy Psychology Techniques for Self-Healing

My web site is www.suehannibal.com.

Association for Comprehensive Energy Psychology, www.energypsych.org, for professional training, an annual conference, peer-reviewed research studies and to find a practitioner locally or who works by phone or Skype.

EFT: www.emofree.com, the site of EFT founder Gary Craig

www.thetappingsolution.com, the site of EFT practitioner Nick Orter and his best-selling book of the same title

www.eftuniverse.com, an extensive site with international resources, books, classes, workshops and practitioner listings

EFT for Combat Stress and PTSD: www.stressproject.org Veterans can obtain six free EFT sessions in exchange for participating anonymously in a study of the efficacy of EFT for PTSD

Documentary showing veterans from Vietnam era through Iraq and Afghanistan healing combat trauma: www.operation-emotionalfreedom.com.

There are dozens of EFT videos on YouTube showing people self-healing various issues. EFT is acupressure tapping on acupoints that correspond to each of the 13 primary meridians combined with some brain balancing techniques. Meridians are energy pathways in the Chinese acupuncture system. Tapping the points while bringing to mind an emotionally charged memory releases the emotional "sting" from the brain. All or part of the memory remains, but there is a feeling of distance from it, a perception of watching it rather than being in it, and other descriptions of detachment or fragmentation. Once treated, the problem doesn't come back, however a subsequent experience can reignite a similar trauma.

TAT, Tapas Acupressure Technique, was invented by Tapas Fleming, a California acupuncturist. TAT is a gentle, elegant technique that involves holding select acupoints on the face with three fingers of one hand while cradling the occiput, (curved portion of back of head) with the other hand. This is called the "pose." Holding the pose while processing a traumatic event or emotional pattern, negative emotions, fears, phobias and other issues through a series of steps neutralizes the traumatic emotional charge and may also release correlated tension or pain from the body.

www.tat-life.com, also on YouTube

Havening is a psychosensory body/mind healing method based on neurological research that shows how Havening touch combined with a series of distraction focused guided imagery prompts releases healing delta waves in the brain. The process changes the recall of a traumatic event by the depotentiation (release) of encoded trauma pathways in the brain. Havening was developed by physician and neuroscientist Ronald Ruden, M.D., Ph.D. Dr. Ruden is also the author of The Craving Brain, and When the Past is Always Present: Emotional Traumatization, Causes and Cures. www.havening.org

Pre-birth and non-verbal trauma, the work of Wendy McCarty, Ph.D., R.N. www.wondrousbeginnings.com

Index

Note: *Names of channeled essays are in italic.*

NOTES

NOTES